Living by Faith

Kenneth R. V. Wheeler

Edited by Steve Wheeler

First published by
Wheelsong Books
4 Willow Close,
Plymouth PL3 6EY,
United Kingdom

Inside illustrations © Steve Wheeler, 2020
Cover photography © Kerry Cole 2020

First published in 2020

Print ISBN 979-8-68495-224-1

Acknowledgements

To my dear late wife Ruth, who encouraged me in all my writing. She injected a spark of hope into my life.

To my son Steve, who presented me with an iPad on my 85th birthday and said "Write your story Dad. There's a story in each of us."

And to Jesus Christ, the author and finisher of my faith.

I hope you enjoy reading these reflections on the Bible as much as I enjoyed writing them. I also hope they will be a blessing to you and will mean something to your life.

God bless you.

Kenneth R V Wheeler
Plymouth
September 2020

Now faith is the substance of things hoped for,
the evidence of things not seen.

(Hebrews 11:1)

Contents

A few words ...

I don't preach in public these days. Our little church building was closed a few years ago, because we had no new pastor to replace the one that left, there was no one to take over the responsibility.

So the powers that be closed the building down and the congregation were scattered to other fellowships in the city. I was so hurt, because our church was no more. It was like a light went out in my life.

That church fellowship had been there for many, many, years. It was the centre of my life. I had such a loving fellowship with the folk in the church, we were very close to them in Christian love.

Suddenly it was all gone and I for one have never fully recovered from that upheaval. The church building was sold and turned into offices. When I think of the family events that took place there, and the great men of God that preached in that church, that filled it to overflowing, where the powerful messages of grace were preached over the years, where many gave their lives to Christ, the pain is almost too much to bear.

When my son Steve bought me an iPad for my 85th birthday it opened up new opportunities to pass on a few words of encouragement to anyone who cared to read my words. I set up a blog on my Facebook page and shared it with the world, and people came to read.

Blogging has been a source of release, a platform for writing a few thoughts each Sunday on my blogs. I have learnt over the years that although church is a place to enjoy fellowship with the saints, the building is just a building.

A more important thing to consider than the building we worship in, is where we stand in God. That is far more crucial to the good of the soul. I can meet with God anywhere and so can you. It's so easy to close your eyes, call upon the Lord, and know He is there listening, caring, and loving. That's what this book is about.

It's about living by faith in God, and believing that He is able to meet your needs where ever you are, and whatever they may be.

I hope you enjoy your own church fellowship, if you are fortunate to be able to attend one, and as you do so I pray that the God of all glory will richly bless you. God bless each and every one of my readers who have taken the trouble to read my blogs and daily devotions.

If you don't attend church, you don't have to do so in order to find serenity. You can still encounter the love of God wherever you are, by calling on the name of Jesus, and you can receive peace and serenity in your life.

Blessings

Kenneth R V Wheeler
Plymouth
September 2020

Trusting in the Father

In Romans 8:28 we read: "For we know that all things work together for good to them that love the Lord, and are called according to His purpose."

There was once a farmer's son who lived in the Swiss mountains. It was summertime and the lad was tending to his father's flock of sheep and goats.

As he did so, he noticed two men who were looking over the side of a ravine with a pair of binoculars. They spotted the lad and waved to him to join them.

They asked the boy if he would mind going down on a rope to collect some alpine flowers that were very rare. Would he dig them out by the roots, put them in a bag, and then they would pull him back up and pay him for his trouble.

The lad looked down and saw that it was a long drop. He turned to the two men and told them that he would have to go home first, to fetch something.

When the lad returned an hour later he was accompanied by a large man. The two men were perplexed, "Why have you brought this man? We wanted you to go down, we couldn't possible lower him up and down, but we could manage you because you are much lighter," they said.

The boy explained, "This is my father, and he will lower me down, and then pull me up."

"Yes, but we could have lowered you down and up between us," said one of the men.

"Yes, I know what you are saying Sir, but I don't know you. But I do know my Father, you see, and I trust that he would never let me fall, because he loves me and I am his only son."

The big farmer lowered his son down over the side of the ravine, and when the lad was ready to come back up, he pulled him back up safely. With the job done the lad received his reward.

As Christians we need to put our trust in our Heavenly Father to see us through any situation we may find ourselves in. We can trust him, because He loves us, and, when we fail and fall down, He is always there to pick us up, to bring us safely back into that place of safety, and if we have called upon the name of Jesus, for His forgiveness.

He will see to it that we shall arrive safely at our heavenly home where we shall receive our reward.

Jairus' daughter

We read in the book of Luke about a man called Jairus who was a ruler of the synagogue. His daughter had fallen ill so he went to Jesus and pleased, "My only daughter is lying at home and she is dying, could you please come and see her!"

It was at this point that as Jesus was making his way to Jairus' house he was interrupted, because a woman in the crowd had touched the hem of His garment (Luke 8:49-55). She was healed of a chronic illness.

While Jesus was talking to her, a man from the house of Jairus arrived and said to him "Your daughter is dead. Don't trouble the Master anymore."

But Jesus said to Jairus, *"Fear not, only believe, and she will be made whole."* Even today, these words of Jesus are so positive so reassuring.

Jesus entered the religious leader's home, and he was immediately greeted by weeping and wailing women, all of whom had probably been paid to be mourners. Jesus said to them, *"Don't cry. She's not dead, she's sleeping."*

The fake mourners laughed at Jesus, because they knew the little girl was dead. But they had no faith, so Jesus put them outside the door.

He took the girl's hand, and told her to rise. Luke 8:55 says her spirit came back into her body and she was brought back to life.

We may have read this particular verse many times but failed to notice its importance. Her spirit had been hovering over her, and when Jesus touched her and spoke, her spirit returned into her. Life was restored. Only believe, the ruler was told.

When our Lord was crucified, after saying in a loud voice *"It is finished,"* He closed his eyes and his spirit left Him. But His spirit hovered over the tomb for three days and nights, when the angels rolled away the stone, His spirit came back, and our Lord was raised again from the dead.

You will recall the time when Jesus asked the sisters Mary and Martha where they had laid the body of their brother Lazarus. They showed Jesus the place, and when He asked them to open the tomb, the bible says Jesus wept.

17

Did you ever stop to think why he wept? I think it was because He was fully aware that this very same thing was going to happen to Him in the coming days. Jesus had an insight of His own death and resurrection.

So, you see how important that verse is to us all. *And her spirit came again.* Up from the grave He arose. Hallelujah, Christ arose.

Your faith has made you whole

I was telling you the story of how Jesus healed the daughter of Jairus. Here's the context for that story:

In the Gospel of Luke 8:43 we read:

"Now a woman having a flow of blood for twelve years, who had spent all her livelihood on physicians and could not be healed by any came from behind and touched the border of His garment. And immediately the flow of blood stopped. And Jesus said "Who touched me?"

This is something to think about. Is Jesus the great healer we make Him out to be?

Yes, of course He is. However, if we read through the scriptures in the four Gospels, especially the events where healings take place, we notice that almost every healing is followed by this phrase from Jesus: *"Your faith has made you whole."*

What Jesus is saying here is, *"It is not my touch, not necessarily my prayer, but your faith in me, that has made you whole. Go and sin no more."* It is the amount of faith we have in Jesus that makes all the difference (Luke 8:43).

Consider the woman we meet in the story. The Bible doesn't mention her by name, but says she had been suffering from haemorrhaging for over twelve years. She spent all her money on doctors, but none of them could stop the bleeding, and slowly but surely it was killing her. She had been informed by others that there was a man of God in the city who was healing people. She had become a desperate woman, and perhaps realised that this might be her last chance.

She was out on the street but, according to the laws of Moses, she was unclean and she should have be isolating. But she was on a mission and she was desperate. She had enough faith to believe that if she could simply touch the hem of His garment, no more than that, it would be sufficient to heal her. She believed this with all her heart.

She saw the large crowd, and in the middle she could see the man of God. She pushed her way through the crowd, and the closer she got to Jesus, the stronger her faith grew. When she was only an arm's length away she dived in and touched the hem of his garments.

Immediately Jesus stopped and asked, *"Who touched me?"*

The disciples were a bit confused. All around him admitted they had not, but as the crowd was very large Peter remarked, *"Master there is a great crowd all around us."*

Jesus insisted, *"Someone touched me, I have perceived that virtue has gone out of me."* Even in such a large crowd Jesus was aware that someone had purposefully touched his clothing. However, he was also fully aware that someone had touched his heart. His great heart of love had been moved with compassion.

The moment the woman touched the hem of his garment she was instantly healed. She was cured of her illness. Jesus was aware someone had touched him he felt divine power leave him and he wanted to know who had received it.

The woman knew she had no way of escaping so she came forward and fell at the feet of Jesus, where she quickly related the story regarding her twelve years of struggle with chronic illness, but added *"The moment I touched you Lord, my troubles were over I was healed."*

Jesus said, *"My daughter, it is your faith that has healed you, now go in peace."*

Jesus didn't say it was your effort, your enthusiasm or your good works or your persistence, that brings healing, but it is your faith that has made you whole.

Over the years, I have heard so many say they have the 'gift of healing.' I would challenge that. I believe it is the measure of faith in Christ people have when they ask for prayer, that brings the healing. Men and women can pray, and there is power in prayer, but it is only in the name of Jesus. There is no other name, not in any Tom, Dick or Harry, that can bring healing. It is the will of God combined with the depth of faith the sick person has that will see them healed.

We are not faith healers, we are healers by faith – the faith we have in Jesus.

Yes, prayer can reach the courts of Heaven, but it's our faith that opens the door.

Faith through prayer

We were at a summer camp in Wales, listening to testimonies. A young man aged sixteen, who had given his life to the Lord only a few days earlier, told the audience of many thousands who were gathered there what had taken place in his life.

The night following his conversion, he went to Swansea's open air market. He was on fire with the joy of receiving his salvation, and he wanted everyone to know. He noticed an older man standing there, so he sidled up to him and said, "Sir, last night I gave my heart and life to Jesus, I want to tell you that Jesus loves you, and he wants you to know him. He wants to be your friend."

The man looked the young boy up and down and said, sceptically, "What do you know son? You haven't see anything of life."

"No you are right, but I'm glad I made a decision to follow Christ, and to live a life pleasing to Him."

The older man then saw an old lady, on two walking sticks hobbling toward them, "Listen boyo, see that woman with two sticks? You talk to her. If your God can heal her, then I will listen to what you have to say," he promised.

The lad told us that the thought crossed his mind at that point that if nothing happened he would look silly, but he took it to be a word from the Lord, so he decided he would go in the name of Jesus.

He walked over to the older lady and stood in front of her.

"Mother, I know I'm only a kid, but I want to tell you God is going to heal you, here and now. Do you believe it?" the lad asked.

Her face lit up, "Do you think you're able to heal me, son?"

"No, but I know a man who can." He had seen many pastors in his church lay hands on people, praying for healing in the name of Jesus. And so he laid his hands on the lady, saying, "In the name of Jesus, I command all your pain to leave you, your infirmity depart in the power of Jesus. You are made whole now, in His name."

He opened his eyes, she had her eyes still closed. "Please give me your sticks," he said to her. Without hesitation she handed them over, and started to walk slowly. People were stopping and watching, making room for her to walk. She started walking faster and faster, then she started to trot. The people started clapping their hands with excitement as she started to run around the market, wearing a great big smile. She returned and thanked the lad.

"Don't thank me, thank the Lord," said the lad. Later he went looking for the old man, but he was nowhere to be seen. He had done a runner.

After his testimony, at the end of the service, one of the pastors, who was asked to close in prayer spoke of how a lady had told him a few minutes ago, (because she had to leave early) that it was her that had received that healing. She had had a dream the night before, and in the dream she was to be healed by a lad called David. The name of that lad was indeed David.

That was in the early 1970s, a long time ago now. But God's power is still just as powerful today. His saints are still active today. All we need is the faith today to believe, and to be available for His service.

God will do the rest.

Faith in action

There was a state in America where the crops were dying in the ground through a lack of rain. So the whole town was asked to come in faith believing with prayer that God would break the drought and send rain to save the crops.

A pastor watched them enter his church, and once everyone was settled down he said, "We can pray all night, but we will not get any rain if you don't have any faith. I watched each and every one of you coming into the building, but there is only of you with any faith, and it's this little girl."

"She was the only one to bring an umbrella." The little girl had enough faith to expect rain when she left home.

Now *that* is real faith in action.

"Truly I tell you, if you have faith as small as a mustard seed, you can say to this mountain, 'Move from here to there,' and it will move. Nothing will be impossible for you." (Matthew 17:20)

Faithful Jesus

Having faith means also being faithful. And there was none more faithful than Jesus.

Jesus said, "I love the Father and whatever the Father commands me to do, I will do. I came down from Heaven not to do my own will, but to do the will of Him who sent me, and the will of Him who sent me is that anyone who sees the Son, and believes on him, will not perish, but have everlasting life." (see John 3:16)

As Jesus was coming up from out of the waters where John had baptised Him, a voice from Heaven declared, "This is my beloved Son, in whom I am well pleased." (Matthew 3:17)

It must have sounded like thunder, but it was the voice of God the Father, making a declaration to the world of His approval for his beloved son, Jesus. God was pleased with Jesus, because he was doing what the father had commanded the son to do.

Oh, that we might hear the voice of the Father saying to us: "This is my child, in whom I am well pleased."

Have we always done what the Lord asked us to do? Have we been faithful servants? Have we obeyed His calling? What do we need to do to become more faithful in God's service?

These are questions we should all ask ourselves if we profess to be Christians.

A flight to Peru

Sometimes we simply need to step out in faith and believe that God has our plans in His hands.

Several years ago I read a story of a young American Christian who said to the Lord, "I will go anywhere you want to send me."

One night God spoke to him in a dream. When the morning dawned, that voice was still ringing in his ears. It said: "Go to the airport and take a flight to Peru."

"But Lord, I don't have any money for a ticket."

"Did I ask you to take money?" was the reply.

So he went with nothing, not even a toothbrush, entered the airport building, and saw a queue for a flight to Lima, so he joined the end, with not a penny to his name. As he moved closer to the ticket office, the man in front of him bought his ticket but just then the man's mobile phone rang and he answered it.

"No, I'll be right there," he said. He turned around.

"Where are you going son?" he asked. The young man told him.

"Good, there's your ticket, all paid for, enjoy your trip," he said, as he ran off.

Right there, that young man learnt a big lesson about faith. On the plane he had a nice meal, and then arrived in Lima, the capital of Peru.

He walked out of the airport, and a taxi driver asked, "You need a taxi, sir?"

"No, I have no money."

"But you need a taxi to get to the church sir."

"How do you know I'm looking for a church?" He asked, surprised.

"God showed me a picture of you in a dream last night, you're to be our new pastor. Jump in. I will take you."

Soon they pulled up outside a tin shack, "Welcome to your church," said the taxi driver. The young man was amazed.

The tin shack was lit by one small light bulb. He could see a small crowd of a dozen people, the only person who could speak English beside himself was the taxi driver.

That church today has expanded into one of the largest Pentecostal churches in South America. He did as he was told, and God saw to his needs. That man was faithful to the Lord and because of his faith, he was blessed beyond measure.

Healed by faith

I remember years ago, when we prayed for the sick, that a brother went to pray for a woman, but she told him, no, she didn't want him to pray for her. She wanted someone else to pray for her, and pointed to me. At that time people thought that it was only pastors and ministers that could do miracles, but Jesus said, so many times in the scriptures, "Your faith has made you whole."

One night I arrived for choir practice too early, when a car pulled up beside me. I saw this new chap. So I invited him to sit in my car whilst we waited for the rest to arrive. I told him about a woman that had received a healing in my church. He was shocked, I found out he was a member of a fellowship that do not believe in healing.

I told him of others that I knew of who had received wonderful healing, we then prayed, and I asked the Lord to open his eyes to the power of God.

The next morning I was in bed, when I heard the phone ringing. I jumped out, raced to the phone, and on the other end there was this man screaming down the phone "It works! It works!"

He had told me how his legs were so painful that he could not walk up the staircase. So, he told me when he got home he read his Bible, and then he said his prayers. He told me what he said in his prayer.

"Lord, if what that chap Ken Wheeler said is true, will you heal my legs." So he did what I told him. He put his hands on his knees and said "I receive my healing in the name of Jesus."

He got up, but nothing had changed, so he went to the stairs, and went up the stairs the only way he could, by sitting on the second step, and pushing himself up the next step until he reached the top.

He went to bed and thought, that's it, there is nothing in it. The next morning he got out of bed walked into the bathroom, started shaving, suddenly it dawned on him, he had walked without any pain.

He went straight to the phone and he was able to walk up and down those stairs, without any discomfort, and that is when he called me and was shouting down the phone, "It works! It works!"

Faith comes by hearing and hearing by the word of God (Romans 10:17).

I spoke the word, and he received a healing by faith, you can do the same thing, open your heart and open your mouth, and see what you can do for the Lord. We can do all things through Christ, who strengthens us.

The faith of Elijah

In 1 Kings chapter 18, we read:

And Elijah said unto Ahab "Get up, eat and drink, for there is a sound of abundance of rain."

So Ahab went up to eat and drink. And Elijah went up to the top of Mount Carmel, and he threw himself down on the ground, and put his face between his knees. And said to his servant, go up now, look toward the sea. And he went up. He looked, and said "there is nothing," and Elijah said, "Go up again. Go up seven times."

It came to pass at the seventh time, that he said. "Behold, there arises a little cloud out of the sea, like a man's hand." And Elijah said, "Go up, say unto Ahab, prepare thy chariot, and get thee down, that the rain stop thee not."

And it came to pass in the meanwhile, that the heaven was black with clouds and wind, and there was a great rain, and Ahab rode, and went to Jezreel.

There had been famine in the land, ever since Elijah had prayed and asked God to hold off the rain, because King Ahab was unfaithful to God.

When he met Elijah, the King asked "Are you he that troubles Israel?" Elijah replied, "I have not troubled Israel but you and your father's household have forsaken the commandments of the Lord."

We all know so many of our friends that have ceased to keep the commandments. They have turned their backs on God, and when things go wrong in their lives, they blame Him.

"You caused the trouble, not me," they will say. But if we read on, we see what happens in the lives of those that turn their back on God, that worship the things of the world. Elijah called down fire from Heaven on the offerings presented to false gods and then it was the end for all those that turned their back on God.

This is a picture of the end of days - which will be the time when Jesus returns.

Peace had returned to Israel, and now that the prophets of Baal had been killed. Elijah wanted to put things back the way they were, so he went to the top of mount Carmel, where he threw himself on the ground, and prayed to his heavenly Father, asking God to send the rains once more to end the famine in the land.

Elijah sent his servant to look out over the sea, to see the first clouds. But the servant came back saying there were none to be seen. So Elijah told him to go back seven times. And on the seventh visit, he returned, reporting that he had seen a small cloud no larger than a man's hand.

How often have we gone and asked for prayer for healing, and nothing happened? We go again, and again, with the same results, so the next time there is a healing invitation in the church, we don't bother to go out, because we have previously been disappointed.

That is the very time we should have gone for prayer. If we pray to the Lord in faith believing, we need to trust Jesus to fulfil his promise to us, that if we ask anything in his name, our heavenly Father will do it. (John 14:14)

Why was there only a very small cloud at first, the size of a man's hand? Because that is the way God works, small at first, but the love of God grows into something so big, that it begins to overflow touching those around us, like when Ahab got the message, the rain was so gentle, but it got heavier and heavier, so that it touched everyone near and far.

The faith of Bartimaeus

In Mark 10:46-52 we read:

Now they came to Jericho. As he went out of Jericho, with his disciples and a great multitude, blind Bartimaeus the son of Timaeus sat by the road begging. And when he heard that it was Jesus of Nazareth he began to cry, "Jesus, son of David, have mercy on me!" Then many warned him to be quiet: but he cried out all the more, "Son of David have mercy on me!"

So Jesus stood still and commanded him to be called. Then they called the blind man saying to him "Be of good cheer. Get up. He is calling you," and, throwing aside his garment, he got up and went to Jesus.

So Jesus said to him, "What do you want me to do for you?" The blind man said to him, "Rabboni, (teacher) that I may receive my sight." Then Jesus said to him "Go your way, your faith has made you well."

We read here of someone who was in a similar sort of situation to the one we found ourselves in during the 2020 pandemic. We were isolated, and so was the blind man.

He had been born sightless, and his name was Bartimaeus. He was isolated in his own dark world, but he did something about it. He had heard that the teacher was passing by, so he shouted out calling to the man of God to take pity on him.

Others tried to silence him, but he shouted more. He was desperate when would he ever get another opportunity to be this close to this mighty man of God.

Jesus heard the cry of this desperate men, "Bring him to me," He commanded. They said to the blind man, "The Master wants to speak with you."

I want you to notice something unusual about the blind man. As soon as he knew he was going to Jesus, he threw his coat onto the ground, before making his way to Jesus. In New Testament times, lepers, or people that were handicapped in any way wore coats of different colours, issued to them by the religious leaders as a warning to the public, to make them aware of the situation.

The blind man threw his coat off, because he had faith to believe that Jesus would heal him, so he would have no further use of it. "What do you want me to do for you?" Jesus asked.

"That I might see again," replied blind Bartimaeus.

"Your faith has made you whole, receive your sight," said Jesus. Immediately the blind man received his sight. Slowly, his sight came to him and then eventually, he was able to see.

Bartimaeus had no hope till he heard about Jesus. He saw no miracle till he called on Jesus. And he had no peace till he believed in Jesus. But he did have faith to believe.

The book of Romans has this verse: *Whosoever shall call upon the name of Jesus, shall be saved* (Romans 10:13).

I have to tell you that this promise has never changed. This promise is open to all mankind, no matter how far you may feel from God, or how low you have sunk in this life. Help is only a prayer away, when we call on the name of Jesus.

How is your faith this morning? Are you desperate enough to call upon the name of Jesus, because He is the only way the truth and the life. No one else can offer you hope, peace, and comfort like Jesus can.

There's more to follow ...

A wealthy member of a church had heard of a pastor who had to give up his ministries through ill health. The pastor had no other income and was now living in poverty.

The rich man found his old pastor's address, put a large sum of money into an envelope and was about to seal it and mail it, when a thought occurred to him. Remembering the old pastor, the rich man knew that if he received a large sum of money, he would give most of it away to help others.

So, the rich man sent a small amount, with a note saying, "More to follow." He knew the heart of that old pastor very well ... but what a lesson there is in that little story.

We may struggle down here with life, but our redeemer and Lord is sending just enough to keep us going. He knows some of us may give it away or waste it, so there is always more to follow, and not just in this life. If we belong to Jesus, there is so much more to follow on the other shore.

There will be the joy of seeing our loved ones again, who have gone before us. They will be there to greet our arrival into eternity, then we will experience that powerful moment that we have been talking and preaching about all our lives. That moment we have anticipated since the scales fell from our eyes, when we first saw the light of salvation. That moment is when we will behold the face of Jesus our Lord in all His risen glory.

Face to face, we will behold Him. It will be worth it all when we see Jesus. Yes, Heaven is going to be a wonderful place.

But our focus will not be on Heaven, or the beauty it possesses, but on the One who made it possible for you and I to be there. He is the one who said, *I go to prepare a place for you, that where I am, there you shall be also.* (John 14:3)

Jesus is the lover of my soul. Yes, there is more to follow, much more then we could ever possibly imagine.

If you don't yet have that assurance, then you need to decide soon, and make that decision to follow Christ.

Immovable objects

You will have tribulations. But be of good cheer, I have overcome the world. (John 16:33)

Years ago men were working on a new bridge across New York city harbour and, when divers were seeking a base for ones of the support towers, they hit a submerged barge that was full of rocks. It had sunk deeply into the mud of the bay.

The divers spent days trying to attach chains to that barge, and tried to lift it, but no crane was powerful enough to do it, that barge was stuck fast out in the mud of the bay.

They called in a specialist engineer who they hoped could solve their problem. He studied the river for a few days, watching its flow.

"When is he going to start doing something?" they asked.

The engineer finally called for two of the largest barges to be brought to the spot, he asked the divers to take the cables from the submerged barge, and attach them to the two floating barges, but not till the tide was at its lowest. As the water start to rise higher and higher, it started to lift the two barges.

The submerged barge responded and it was released from the mud of the harbour floor. It had been done by the power of the ocean tide. The engineer allowed the floating barges to be carried up the harbour by the incoming tide, away from the place where the tower was to stand.

Likewise, in our Christian walk, lives that are mired in sin are raised out of their plight by the Holy Spirit's heavenly power. When helped by His power, they find a release from debilitating sinful habits that keep them down in the deep mud and away from God's fullness.

The ability to break free from sin and to live the way we should, is not found in our own willpower or energy or thinking. But the source of our strength is in our creator and redeemer who will lift us out of the miry clay, allowing us to flow to a place of peace and safety.

With the psalmist we can say with triumph, *Power belongs to the Lord.* (Psalm 62:11)

So if you have some unmovable object like a bad habit in your life, that is causing you to stray away from the path that God has for you to walk, and, if everything you have tried will not remove it.

Then turn your problem over in your prayers to the great Engineer in the Heavens, God Himself will then watch the unmovable object be released floating away out of harm's way.

If you do this, you will be able to live the life that God has chosen for you.

If God is for us ...

God never lets His children down. The Bible promises this:

The Lord is with you, never again will you fear any harm, He is mighty to save, He will deal with all who oppress you. (Isaiah 54:17)

God promises to live with His people, and to save them from their enemies:

The Lord hath taken away thy judgment, he hath cast out thine enemy: the King of Israel even the Lord is in the midst of thee: thou shalt not see evil any more. The Lord thy God in the midst of thee is mighty; He will save, he will rejoice over thee with joy: he will Joy over thee with singing. (Zephaniah 3:15-17)

God calls us to be courageous and to trust in Him:

Be strong and courageous, do not be afraid nor dismayed for the Lord thy God is with you. My soul finds rest in God alone; my salvation comes from him. He is my fortress, I shall never be shaken. (2 Chronicles 32:7)

We need not worry about anything. Instead, we should pray about everything. You can tell God your needs. If you do this you will be at peace with God.

Here is a scripture that sums it all up from the book of Romans:

Neither principalities, nor powers, nor things present, nor things to come. nor heights, not depth, nor any other creature, shall be able to separate us from the love of God, which is in Christ Jesus our Lord. (Romans 8:48-39)

Are you fully persuaded today, that nothing can separate you from the love of God?

Do you have faith that He will always do what He promises?

Trouble on all sides

Jesus never said that if we follow Him there will be no troubles. Paul writes to the Corinthian church:

We are troubled on every side, yet not distressed; we are perplexed, but not in despair; persecuted, but not forsaken; cast down, but not destroyed; we are troubled on all sides. (2 Corinthians 4:8-9)

How many of us are feeling that way? Similarly to the Coronavirus pandemic, we are unable to see what we are up against. Our enemy is invisible. So we have a tendency to feel vulnerable, thinking that the enemy is all around us on every side. We feel overwhelmed. Yet, like Paul and the disciples, we should not be distressed.

Think of those words of the scripture: *I will not give you more than you can handle, or that you can cope with.* (1 Corinthians 10:13) That is why, like Paul, we need not be distressed. God has your best interests at heart.

The scripture also says, "We are perplexed." The dictionary defines perplexed as meaning over burdened with worry, bewildered because we don't know what's happening around us, to be confused and puzzled. How many times do we feel exactly like that?

During the pandemic we have been confined, isolated, many of us living for long periods in solitude. We have been unable to do our normal activities such as visiting friends and family. Such a situation would make most people a little perplexed.

But the scripture goes on to say, *Yet we are not in despair. It means we have not given up, we are still in the fight, we are not worried, we are not going to let the situation over burden us. Because we know who is in control, and in faith believing we will continue to put our trust in our Saviour.*

Even if the worst should happen, what do we really have to fear? If you belong to Him, you need to remember that Jesus has overcome death and the grave, he has prepared a home in the glory for His own.

Praise be to God who has blessed us with all spiritual blessings. So we do not need to be in despair, our faith in Christ will see us through any situation if we continue to put the Him at the steering wheel of our life.

A peaceful mind

In my dreams one night all sorts of things passed through my mind. Some I did not want to see, and I certainly didn't want to linger upon them, but they would not go away. In the end, I had to call on the name of the Lord, to drive it away and set my mind free. I kept repeating that scripture we find in Paul's letter to the Philippians:

Let this mind be in you, which is also in Christ Jesus (Philippians 2:5)

There is another scripture that says that we are transformed by the renewing of our minds. (Romans 12:2)

When we come to salvation, we receive a new heart, a new nature in Christ, we also receive the spirit of Christ in our hearts. This is a renewal of the mind. So often, the mind is overlooked.

Furthermore, we can find our minds are often like a stagnant pool of water, when our mind should be like a fresh flowing river of sweet water that is good to drink, pure and wholesome. Our minds should be where our dreams become a blessing, and where we can find ourselves in the presence of the Lord.

He will often break in on our minds, to encourage us in our journey of faith. But our Lord is not going to visit us in our minds and dreams if they are nothing more than stagnant pools of filthy water.

Can you see the point I am trying to make? This is why it is so important to continually have a renewal within our minds, and ensure that it is kept out of bounds to the devil and his demons. Then we will be able to sleep and dream in peace without any anxiety.

Do not conform to the pattern of this world, but be transformed by the renewing of your mind. Then you will be able to test and approve what God's will is — his good, pleasing and perfect will. (Romans 12:2-3)

In the war zone

Be strong in the Lord, and in the power of His might. (Ephesians 6:10)

Today, while many are falling away from the faith and the presence of evil seems to be everywhere we look, this scripture is so important to us. Christians are required to stand in the power of His might, especially in these final days, days that are so full of evil intention that is happening before our very eyes.

Ephesians 6:12 tells is that we are in a battle, a war zone. The verse indicates that we are fighting not against people but against evil forces, and the wickedness in high places. It's a battle between purity of the mind or surrender to sinful nature. Most battles are fought in the mind and we need to keep a constant watch on what enters our minds. It is so important in these last days to keep vigilant.

What do you think the phrase 'wickedness in high places' might mean?

I believe that all over the world there are wicked minded people in places of authority, in government, in parliament, in the United Nations and the European Council. Such people are being manipulated by evil forces, and some are engaged in pagan worship.

Never in the history of our world have we had such darkness or such an upheaval of wickedness as we have today. The minds of many in authority have been pierced by the evil darts of the enemy of our souls.

We know this because we read:

In whom the god of this world hath blinded the mind of them that believe not, lest the light of the glorious Gospel of Christ, who is the image of God the Father should shine into them. (2 Corinthians 4:4)

In Ephesians 6:11 we as believers are commanded to put on the whole armour of God, so that we can stand firm in the evil days and having done all, we are able to survive with our faith intact.

2 Cor 10:4 says: *For the weapons of our warfare are not carnal, but mighty to the pulling down of strongholds.*

It's our obedience in Christ that will win the battle and make us victors in this war zone, not the evil of the prince of darkness.

We need to put on, or adopt the following items of 'armour' if we are to be battle ready:

- The breastplate of righteousness
- Wearing the shoes of the Gospel of peace
- The shield of faith
- The helmet of salvation
- The sword of the spirit.

Verse 17 says: *Finally my brethren be strong in the Lord and in the power of His might.*

We are not called to be strong in our own strength, but in the power and majesty of the King of Kings and Lord of Lords.

Do not fear

We are living through fearful times, but it won't last forever. There will come a great day in human history when Jesus returns to Earth. When the sound of the last trumpet echoes across the universe, all who hear the sound of His voice, every person in Heaven and Earth – and that includes all the angels and demons, and even Satan himself – will humbly fall to their knees, because the scripture says that

...at the name of Jesus every knee should bow, of those in heaven, and of those on earth, and of those under the earth, and that every tongue should confess that Jesus Christ is Lord, to the glory of God the Father. (Philippians 2:10-11)

In 1 John 4:18 we read: *There is no fear in love, perfect love casts out fear.* Where else can you find such comfort in this time of uncertainty?

Give your worries and cares over to the Lord. Call upon His name, and ask for peace to soothe your troubled soul. It's time to release the pressure valve and let Jesus take over.

We are all fully aware that we are living in a rapidly changing sequel of events. Where fear and panic is prevalent amongst us.

If we are the children of God, we should be above any fear. If you and I have the love of God embedded within our lives, fear should be the last thing on our minds because perfect love casts out all fear

Threats such as pandemics must surely come from the evil one himself, to cause panic and fear in the hearts and lives of God's people.

How do we approach the throne of mercy? Do we come full of the boldness in the Lord, or do we approach him in fear and trembling?

Yes, terrible things may be happening all around us, where so many are losing their lives or their incomes and there is much sorrow. However, the word of hope to all of us from God still stands strong today, especially for the situation we currently find ourselves in:

I will never leave you or forsake you. (Hebrews 13:5)

That is a message of real faith and hope.

A confidence booster

What do we have to fear? If we have committed our hearts and lives to the Lord Jesus, and if we are washed in His blood and are filled by His spirit, then we belong to Him. We are not our own, we have been purchased with a price, the price of His shed blood.

So whether we live or whether we die, we still belong to Him.

Let us be mindful that our Heavenly Father can take any disastrous situation, or any act of wickedness, and turn it around for good. So many people who have never paid any attention to their sinful lives, or given a thought about turning to God, are now on their knees calling out for forgiveness, and salvation, and this is going on all over the world today.

Can you say with me now, I belong to Jesus, not for the years of time alone, but for eternity?

That's why fear should have no grip on a child of the living God, if we truly belong to Jesus. Then we are members of the Courts of Heaven, no matter what takes place.

Unusual times

We are living in an unusual time, when all around us seems to be in darkness. The world would appear to be out of control, with no one seemingly at the helm steering the ship.

Let's make it plainly understood from the start that this is a lie of the enemy. He is casting confusion and dismay into every heart, and is trying to block the light of God from shining into this dark world. But God is in control.

It is our business to shine forth, to shine for Jesus, you see, Light dispels darkness. In the early days of sailing ships, they could be at sea in total darkness racing toward rugged rocks, that would cause them to hit and sink. But a lighthouse would shine its light into the darkness, warning the captain so he could then steer his ship away from the dangerous rocks.

And that is the reason we need to shine the light of Christ into this dark world around about us, to warn weary men and women that they are heading to a place where they may very well end up on the rocks of utter despair.

I can feel there are those who are asking, what good is my little light? In such a vast, dark world, they will not notice my feeble light. Well, let me remind you that the great fire of London – which almost destroyed the entire city – was caused by a single candle. That's all it takes, just a small spark to set fire to an entire city.

Or perhaps to save a nation, because Jesus said: *I am the light of the world.* (John 8:12)

That statement still stands strong today. Because His spirit is resident in everyone who has accepted Jesus Christ as their lord and saviour. We should be each a shining example of Christ. His light should be shining out in our daily lives, if we are still walking in the light of salvation.

Are we still shining our light, or have we hidden it 'under a bushel' so that it is hidden from view?

May the lord of all glory shine on you, filling you with all joy and contentment, so that we may shine with the love of Christ in our work and play.

If we have Christ in us we should glow as we reflect His glory to attract others into His kingdom.

Winning through faith

The Bible says: *I can do all things through Christ who strengthens me.* (Philippians 4:13)

A man once asked a pastor "If I give my life to Jesus, will all my problems go away?"

The pastor replied, "It's not that easy, I'm afraid. Jesus won't take your problems away, but He will give you wisdom and power to deal with them."

The pastor was right.

God will give us divine courage, give us brothers and sisters to help us in our in our walk with Christ, and bring the people of God into our lives who can support and inform us.

An athlete will never be a winner until she learns to lose gracefully. Only then she will find she has the resilience to win. But first she has to overcome the fear of losing.

If God took away all our problems from us all at once we would be calling on God to do everything for us, and this would leave us useless and defenceless, unequipped to resist the enemy of our soul.

God says: *I will never leave you or forsake you* (Deuteronomy 31:6).

We can always depend on that promise, but there are times when He will put us in a position where we need to sort out things on our own.

However, we know that God will never allow us to fight any battle or face any challenge without granting us the power to overcome the enemy.

There is power in the name of Jesus. The name of Jesus can be your weapon to defeat your enemy and send him running.

At the name of Jesus every knee should bow, of those in heaven, and of those on earth, and of those under the earth, and that every tongue should confess that Jesus Christ is Lord, to the glory of God the Father. (Philippians 2:10-11)

Coping with depression

The story of the prophet Elijah is inspirational, especially for those who may be dealing with depression.

In 1 Kings, chapter 18 we read that Elijah is in full control of the situation. He has called down fire from the Heavens to burn up a sacrifice, to show that God's power is greater than that of any of the pagan gods. He then took the prophets of the false god Baal, not allowing one of them to escape, to the Brook Kidron and there he had them executed.

After that he went up to the top of Mount Carmel and cast himself down on the ground. He was worn out, so he told his servant boy, "Go up and see if there is any sign of rain out over the sea," The boy returned to report there were no clouds in the sky. Seven times he sent him up to look, it was only on the seventh time that the boy returned to say he could see a cloud the size of a man's hand. His words were, "I saw a cloud arise from the sea like a man's hand."

It was what Elijah was waiting for – the hand of God to appear. You see without God's approval, he could do nothing. I want to tell each and every one of you reading this, that we too can do nothing without of good without the approval of the Almighty. So many have tried to do it on their own, myself included, and we failed or had only limited success. But if we had God's blessing, it would have been mission fulfilled every time.

We find our hero of the day, having seen the glory of God and his power. The very same man is no longer powerful, victorious, or brave but no, he is running away in fear for his life, because of a threat from a woman. In chapter 19:2 we read that Queen Jezebel sent a messenger to Elijah.

She had by now received the news that all her prophets had been put to the sword by Elijah, and she sends him an angry message, *"Let the gods do to me, and more also, if I make not thy life as the life of one of them by tomorrow, about this time."*

Elijah was suddenly filled with fear as he hears this. Only hours ago he was afraid of nothing and no-one, because he had God's anointing. Now, instead of waiting on His God, he panicked and ran away in fear.

And this is what so many of us have done when we come up against something that scares us. We lose sight of God, and we find ourselves like Elijah, panicking and fearful instead of waiting on God's provision.

Elijah ran to the Beersheba, about a day's journey into the wilderness, in a state of fear. He found a juniper tree to sit under, out of the heat of the sun, and there, in his depression, he waited to die. What do people do when then fall into a state of depression? Often they say, "I want to end it all. I can't take any more."

Elijah had lost the anointing that God placed on him. He had been given power, authority and a direct line into the throne room of God. And it was only now he thought about talking to God, but it was a request that he might be allowed to die: "It is enough now, O Lord, take away my life, for I am no better than my father."

How many of you have been in that same situation? We have come to the end of the road, we have come up against a brick wall and we want to pack it in. I have known a few pastors like that, and they have left the ministry that the Lord had given them. They were so full of anointing and wanted to be the very best for God, to proclaim the promise of Christ to all the nations of the world. But where are they now? They are sitting under their juniper trees, out of touch with God, defeated and depressed.

Did you notice what happened next in verse six? Elijah found food to eat, and water to drink, and later an angel came and brought more food and water for him. In effect, the angel was saying "Come on, buck yourself up. God has something for you to do, and it's a long journey."

And that is what the Lord is saying to all of us that are depressed and downcast "I'm not finished with you yet. Eat up the word of truth, drink the waters that speak of the Holy Spirit, and be prepared for another journey in my name. This time if you closely follow me, and do what I have equipped you for, you will not fail. I will never leave you or forsake you. You will always be mine."

Sir Winston Churchill, who experienced depression, once said: "When you are going through hell….. keep going!"

Depression is a terrible thing to go through, but you need to know that God has a purpose for you, so keep going!

Don't worry about anything

Philippians 4:4 says this:

Rejoice in the Lord always. Again I will say, rejoice! Let your gentleness be known to all men. that the Lord is at hand. Be anxious for nothing, but in everything by prayer and supplication, with thanksgiving let your requests be made known to God. And the peace of God, which surpasses all understanding will guard your hearts and minds through Christ Jesus. Finally brethren, whatever things are true, whatever things are noble, whatever things are just, whatever things are pure, whatever things are lovely, whatever are of good report, if there is any virtue and if there is anything praiseworthy, meditate on these things.

The Apostle Paul wrote:

I have learned in whatever state I am in to be content. I can do all things through Christ who strengthens me. (Philippians 4:11-13)

Are we rejoicing in this path we find ourselves on, or are we still worrying and concerned about all that is going on around us? We are told in the scriptures not to worry about anything. We should take whatever is troubling us to God's throne and leave it there, *for greater is He that is in us, than he that is in the world.* (1 John 4:4)

Jesus said: *My peace I leave with you, not as the world would give, but an abiding peace, that is satisfying and will calm your fears.* (John 14:27)

It's only when we realise and understand that when we surrendered our hearts and lives into the care of our lord and saviour Jesus Christ, that we ceased to be members of this world, this is no longer our home, we are just passing through.

Our homes are in Glory, where sin and fear are illegal. Have you ever thought about that?

Contentment is a form of peace. Are we contented with our lives and our service for Him?

The importance of peace

The Lord Jesus used peace to still a sudden storm that had blown up as they were crossing the Sea of Galilee.

Jesus said: "Peace. Be still!" and the tempest had no option but to obey. The wind ceased to blow, the angry waves lost their power, and the fearful hearts of the fishermen became calm once again. (Mark 4:39)

Is your heart still? your mind untroubled and at peace. If so, you are very fortunate, because so many Christians today are without the joy of having this abiding peace and satisfaction in their hearts. Why is this?

It's because they are not at peace. They don't have that perfect rest that the Lord Jesus promised us we can receive. *My Peace, I give unto you.* (John 14:27)

May I be so bold as to state something that so few of us know. That peace is a part of our worship! A silent heart and an untroubled mind is so hard to maintain in this day and age, because of noise, stress, pressures, distractions and the fear of the unknown. One of the ploys of the evil one is to steal the peace we all should possess. He is out to destroy the peace of each and every believer.

You cannot pray if you cannot find total peace in your own heart and soul.

Be still

The Bible says, "Be still and know that I am God," or it could be translated as, "Be at peace and know that I am God." (Psalm 46:10)

That is why the enemy is out to steal our peace. It is only in the stillness that we will locate God the Father, and find ourselves.

Ask yourself this question: When was the last time you communed in sweet fellowship with your Lord, without your prayers being interrupted by evil thoughts, or your thoughts bombarded with uselessness? It's the ploy the enemy uses most to rob us of our peace.

I read a story of a mother who was on holiday with her family in Scotland. They had to stay there because of the coronavirus pandemic. After a few days the little girl said mummy, "Mummy, I've gone deaf."

The mummy replied, "No you haven't darling, it's called stillness, all is at peace."

Dealing with a blockage

Have you ever felt cut off from God's blessing?

This can sometimes happen in the Christian spiritual life because there is a blockage or a restriction in the flow of God's blessing. So often we find a blockage can interfere with our Christian walk.

When there is no longer any joy in your service, your heart and soul grows hard. Where you could once pray with ease, it now becomes a chore or a burden.

When you read the Word of God it no longer has that revealing factor, nor does it have that quality of satisfaction and the word fails to come alive to you. Those around you still have the joy of their salvation, yet you feel dried up.

You no longer have that zeal you once had for the work of the master, now you feel left outside, alone. It could be something blocking the blessing of God in your life.

My drainage at home was once blocked during a heavy storm. The rain was collecting in the downpipes from the roof, so the rain on the roof, in the guttering began flowing down the side of the house, and all this was caused by a blocked up drain.

Once I pulled the dead leaves out, the water started flowing down through the downpipe freely into the drains.

A blockage need not be something big. It can be just a simple thing, or something small and insignificant that can lead to a blockage.

King David was cut off from the blessing of God because he

did something selfish that caused the death of an innocent man in battle. It wasn't long before David was shouting to God *"Lord, return to me the joy of my salvation."* (Psalm 51:12)

He had a blockage which had cut off God's blessing and grace.

If you are feeling cut off from the grace of God and from the joy of your salvation, may I suggest you return to the source where all our blessings began.

It's the place where we had our first encounter with the Lord Jesus, where we received our salvation. It's right there at the foot of the cross. It was His atoning blood that set us free from sin, and it is still the source of a blessing today.

What we need to do, is to remove our eyes off the blockage putting them back on the Saviour, gaze upon his face, then the blockage will clear, and the blessings will start to flow again.

This is often the case with sickness. We are so busy focusing on the symptoms of our illness and how we feel, that we fail to see the face of the healer and restorer of our blessings, Jesus Christ Himself.

You will come across many blockages in your journey of faith. But the answer to the problem is always the same – return to the source, to the beginning, because Christ is the answer to our every need. It's important never to allow anything to come between you and the Lord.

No emotions, no fear, no tragedies, no experiences, nothing must be allowed to separate us or cause a blockage or restriction of the flow of God's blessing. With God's blessings we are protected, we are maintained, we are empowered, we are fortified in our daily endeavours. Without it we are exposed.

We are required to keep the channels clear, so God's blessings can freely flow into our lives and we can have a victorious Christian life, walking in faith.

Persecuted for faith

Blessed are they which are persecuted for righteousness sake, for theirs is the Kingdom of Heaven. (Matthew 5:10)

All over the world there are millions of people that are becoming Christians. In countries hostile to the Gospel they are often persecuted, imprisoned, and in some cases, even murdered for their faith.

Their churches are burned or destroyed, or bulldozed to the ground. They battle on in the strength of the Lord. They don't give up and move away. They carry on steadfastly, to build another place of worship and continue proclaiming the good news that Christ is still the only way to salvation.

It's the life they live that attracts others to the Cross.

Today, even in western nations, Christians are being persecuted in their work, universities and schools, and even in the home. Even their own family members can be against them, because of their faith in Jesus.

If you think you have nothing to pray for, try praying for Christians in countries like North Korea, China, Iran, Pakistan, and many other countries, who are imprisoned because of their faith. Some have been in prison for many years, and are prepared to die, rather than deny Christ or abandon their faith in Him.

The Word of God has plenty to say about the persecuted church:

Blessed are they when men shall revile them and persecute them, and shall say all manner of evil against them falsely for my sake. (Matthew 5:11).

Rejoice, and be exceedingly glad: for great is your reward in heaven; for such were persecuted of the prophets, which were before you. (Matthew 5:12)

In Matthew 5:14 Jesus asks us not to hide our faith: *You are the light of the world. A city that is set on a hill cannot be hid.*

Jesus exhorts us to stand tall for his kingdom: *Let your light so shine before men, that they may see your good works: and glorify your Father which is in Heaven* (Matthew 5:16).

Those that are faithful in the persecuted church can be assured of the riches of the kingdom of Heaven and the blessings of God the Father. Great joy will be their reward just like that given to the prophets of old or the early Christian church.

The light that the persecuted church is shining can be seen by the whole wide world. It cannot be hidden away or extinguished. It's like a city on a hillside. (Matthew 5:14) It's the light in the world shining down through the avenues of time and history and by it, mankind will always obtain eternal life and salvation.

Enjoy the freedom you have to walk into a church and worship without persecution. Remember to give thanks that you are still at liberty to do so. And remember to pray for those who can't.

A loving embrace

I recently attended the funeral of a nephew in law. His dear wife looked so sad, and I knew just how she was feeling. I had gone through the same thing only a couple of months earlier when I lost my dear wife Ruth. Later when I had a chance to be alone with my niece I drew her into my arms and hugged her. I said very little, because that hug spoke for itself.

When I was ministering years ago I remember not long after I had conducted a funeral, the widow was in a bad way. I hugged her, and she burst into tears, and said, "The thing I miss most are my husband's hugs."

I never fully understood what she was saying at that time, till years later I found myself in that same position. Suddenly what she had said was so true. The thing you miss more than anything else, is being hugged. It's not the sound of their voice, or their smile, nor their very presence.

Yes, all of them you would love to hear and see, but it's no longer possible. However, a hug is a different matter. It brings with it the feeling of security, tenderness, and compassion. Hugs are like a tenderising salt that you put on steaks to make them softer, to remove the tension in the fibres.

It's very much like this when a child is born and the first thing it feels is the fresh air entering its lungs. The next thing the child experiences is the loving embrace of the mother. That first hug is so crucial, so necessary in the bonding of a mother to child and child to mother, because it implants into the child's memory. That hug of abundance security, of tenderness of mercy, that feeling of being wanted and loved.

And at the time of deep hurt and suffering after the departure of someone dear, your feelings are much like that of a new born baby. You're feeling alone, vulnerable, unsettled, till you feel the arms of love wrapped around you holding you close. It gives you that feeling of security, of tenderness and love and with that embrace comes the feeling that someone loves you, wants you, that they feel for you.

It's called compassion, be it your son or daughter brother or sister, friend or a relative. Those hugs are what are so important and so necessary to install a barrier of an unbreakable love.

I once saw a remarkable painting of a young lady weeping, standing beside the grave of her husband. The artist had painted an image of Jesus, with his arms embracing that dear girl comforting her.

I know that my Saviour and Lord is ever ready to embrace any troubled soul. One touch from the Master, and you'll be like that child I was talking about. You will receive a new life in Jesus Christ.

One touch from the Master is all it takes.

Salvation and redemption

For there is only One God and only one mediator between God and men, the man Christ Jesus. (1 Timothy 2:5)

We have been redeemed by the precious blood of the Lamb. (1 Peter 1:28-19)

Years ago in the United Kingdom, we had pawn brokers in almost every street.

My dear mother and every mother that I knew who lived in our area, would take their husband's best suit, or his watch, or anything precious they might own, and would take it along to the pawnbroker to obtain a small loan till payday came along.

A few days later, they would return to the pawn brokers to buy it back, they would have to pay more money to get it back than they borrowed. It was called redeeming. It meant to buy back what was already your own. It's so precious that you want it back and you are willing to pay a price for it.

When I was a child I would hear people talk about uncle Jack, and for a long time, I thought that we had a rich uncle I had never met. It turned out to be the nickname for pawnbrokers.

In the area of Plymouth where I grew up, everyone was poor and lived from hand to mouth. With so many children (there were eleven of us) there was never enough money coming in.

We used to eat well enough, because we had a mother who was a great cook, and an allotment where our Dad grew most of what we ate. But most weeks mother had to visit uncle Jack.

And this is what God did for each and every one of us. We were lost and sold into slavery of sin, we were without hope. We had all been born in pureness without a spot or blemish. But as we grew older, we started to turn away from the love of God that was in us. The Bible reminds us of our fallen state:

We have all sinned and we have all fallen short of the glory of God. (Romans 3:23)

We turned away from the path of righteousness, doing our own thing, going our own way, allowing the enemy to come in and take procession of our very souls. (Isaiah 53:6)

Because of this sin and deliberate disobedience to God's laws, the entire human race is under an eternal condemnation. In Romans 6:23 we read that *the wages of sin is death, but the gift of God is eternal life.*

God still loves us no matter what we have done. He was determined to buy each of us back to bring us back into the fold. He did this through Christ's death on a Roman cross.

Jesus paid the full ransom that would redeem us. His death was to buy us back, so we could again belong to Him. He loved us so much that He was willing to die a sinners death on the cross of Calvary in our place, and His death paid the full price of our salvation.

I trust that everyone reading this can say they have been redeemed by the blood of the Lamb.

Taking the punishment

This story happened many years ago but it still has a message for us today. The year was 1943. The story is about a French train driver who had been working away for two days and arrived home to find his wife crying. He asked her what was wrong.

She told him "Our son Pierre was caught by the Germans as he was placing explosives on the railway lines, and they are going to shoot him."

The father, still in uniform, rushed to the police barracks and asked to speak to the German commander. He was shown to an office where he removed his hat and entered.

He began, "Sir, I am the father of Pierre Laval. He is our only son, he is only a boy, he knows nothing about the war, can you please let him come home with me. I will punish him, his poor mother is suffering because of him." he pleaded.

"I am sorry, the death warrant for him has already been issued and signed, I can't rescind it," the German officer said, "The death sentence must be carried out. Those are my orders and there is nothing I can do for him." He showed the death warrant to the Father.

The father spent some time reading it.

"Sir, in France the first son born is always given the name of the Father, the name on here is also my name, Pierre Laval. Can you not set my son free, and I will take his place?"

The German officer thought for a moment, and then he said "It makes no difference as long as the crime is paid for. If you are willing to die in your son's place I can arrange it. May I say you're a true Frenchman, one who is prepared to die so that your son may live." He picked up the phone and spoke. A few minutes later his son entered the room. The boy ran to his father and they hugged. "I'm sorry to bring such trouble to your door, father."

The father held his son at arm's length, "I want you to promise me, you will never do anything like this again."

"I promise, I will not do such a thing again, father."

"Then you can go home now and bring comfort to your mother."

"I can go home?" said the lad, looking toward the officer, who waved his hand for the lad to leave. He kissed his father and said, "I will wait outside for you father."

"No, Pierre. Go directly home to your mother, she needs comfort, and she's waiting for you."

The boy left the room, and his mother was delighted to have her son home, but she still wondered where her husband was.

Later that night, the peace of the evening was disturbed by the noise of guns firing. The father had been executed. He has given his life to save his only son.

This is what happened to Jesus, he became our substitute – for you and I, and for the whole world. Just like the father in the story, he went willingly to die in our places so that we might have new life.

God can't stand to look at sin. But we are all sinners, so there is a huge barrier, a gulf between us and our creator. Without the shedding of blood, there can be no remission of sin (Hebrews 9:22). Every one of us is guilty of sin, but because of the cleansing blood of the Lamb of God, we can be seen as pure and without sin in the sight of a Holy God.

Right now you may be asking: What do I need to do to become a Christian, so I can receive this new life?

John 3:16 is probably the most famous verse in the Bible. It says: "*God so loved the world, that He gave his only begotten Son, that whosoever believes in Him will not perish, but will have everlasting life.*"

Talk to someone who believes what the Bible says and has a strong faith. There must be someone near to you. Ask them to lead you to the Saviour.

For when we were still without strength, in due time, Christ died for the ungodly. For scarcely for a righteous man will one die: yet perhaps for a good man, one might even dare to die. But God demonstrates His own love toward us, in that while we were yet sinners, Christ died for us. Much more then, having now been justified by His blood, we shall be saved from wrath through Him (Romans 5:6-9).

Forgiven

For God made Christ, who never sinned, to be the offering for our sin, so that we could be made right with God through Christ. (2 Corinthians 5:21)

During my time as an elder in the church, after most meetings we would encourage anyone that needed prayer to come to the front. One dear old soul would come out most times for the same thing, asking for forgiveness for past sins. I thought she must have done something truly awful, because all the talking and praying was of no use to her.

"But you have been forgiven by the blood of the lamb," I would say.

Yes, she admitted she knew that but she would not, or could not, forgive herself. I never found out what it was she had done or said until several years later, at her funeral.

It was then a relative told me that when she was just seventeen years old she had fallen pregnant, which in those days was seen as a shameful act of sinful living.

So she went to a back street doctor and had an abortion, and that was the reason she could never forgive herself. The baby was a little girl, and every night she would imagine she saw that little girl standing by her bedside, looking at her.

What a weight of guilt that was to bear each and every day of her long life.

She never knew what it was to smile, and nothing she was told could bring any her peace or happiness. She had given herself a guilty verdict on her crime, and she carried that prison sentence with her for the rest of her life.

We don't need to wonder if we've been forgiven, we don't need to carry around a burden of guilt of memories of yesterday faults, "If we confess our sins, He (Jesus) is faithful and just to forgive all our sins, and to cleanse us from all unrighteousness." (1 Corinthians 5:21)

No matter whether the sin is big or small, those who belong to Him have been washed in His blood. No matter what the severity of the sin, they have been saved and forgiven.

God's antidote for sin

And the people spoke out against God (Numbers 21).

The Israelites had been wandering in the desert for a long time and they were complaining about the shortage of food and water. They were unhappy about having to eat nothing by the manna that was supplied by God fresh every morning.

God sent a plague of snakes among the bitter and complaining people, and when they were bitten, many of them died. They quickly got the message and remembered they had spoken against God. They became aware that they had sinned.

So they went to Moses, admitting to him that they had sinned, and begged Moses to ask the Lord to remove the poisonous snakes from among them. They were full of repentance. Most people are, when there is a price to pay.

God would not remove the snakes, but He did offer an antidote. He instructed Moses to make a fiery serpent out of brass, place it on a pole, and lift it high in the middle of the camp. If anyone was bitten by a poisonous snake they only had to look up at the serpent of brass, and they would live.

This deliverance from sin described in the book of Numbers is a foreshadowing (prophecy) of Christ's crucifixion. Jesus Himself referred to it when He said *"If I be lifted up from the Earth, I shall draw all men unto me."* (John 12:32)

This is a picture of the pathway so many of us walked to find our salvation. We saw Calvary's cross high and lifted up with our Lord crucified upon it.

Just like those bitten by poisonous snakes, we had been infected by the toxic sins of this world, doomed to die as sinners, and then to be separated from God for eternity. God's antidote for sin is the death and resurrection of His Son, as a substitute for the punishment we all deserved.

And just as the Israelites looked up in faith to the brass serpent on the pole, we looked up and saw the Jesus on that cross. He died to take away our sin so that we would be able to live again. That's an effective antidote. That's faith.

You and I have been drawn by the love of God, out of death and the grave that awaited us.

One day we shall spend eternity with the saints and the one who made it all possible, Jesus the Lamb of God, who takes away the sins of the world.

One mediator

Here are two great verses from the Bible:

Now, unto the King eternal, immortal, invisible, the only wise God, be honour and glory for ever and ever. Amen. (1 Timothy 1:17)

Who would have all men to be saved, and to come unto the knowledge of the truth. For there is only One God. And only one mediator between God and men, the man Christ Jesus. (1 Timothy 2:5)

The world says 'God is dead'. But our God cannot be dead, because He is eternal and immortal. This means He cannot die, unlike so many in the world who worship graves and dry dead bones of their so called gods, we worship a Living God. There is an empty tomb just outside of Jerusalem. Jesus is alive. We can hold a conversation with Him, He answers our prayers, He understands our problems and He appreciates and accepts our praise.

Yes, God is invisible, but that's because He is Spirit. However, we can feel His presence, hear His voice, put our trust in Him to take care of us when we call upon His name. As the scriptures say, He is the only wise God.

The scripture goes on to say He is to be praised and honoured, forever. I'm sure that Heaven is flooded with the praise and worship of the millions the world, that have surrendered their hearts and lives to His call of salvation. They have been saved through the death and resurrection of Jesus Christ.

He ransomed us from a state of despair, washing us clean from sin and corruption. He was crucified on a cross of shame, shedding his own blood, so that you and I can stand sinless and faultless before His Holy Father on high. And on that great day, that is yet to come, every knee will bow and every tongue confess, that Jesus Christ is Lord of all (Philippians 2:10-11)

That is why the second scripture is added: That there is only *one* God and *one* mediator between man and God, that is the man Christ Jesus. Jesus was God in human form. That is why He is able to mediate between man and God. Only Jesus could achieve this.

No one can stand before the only wise God, in any other name, except in the name of Jesus. He alone has the authority, the power and the righteousness to grant us entry into the very presence of His Holy Father. Have you made that call yet or are you still unsure of your salvation? If you haven't, do call upon the name of Jesus, and you will be saved.

The sinner's prayer

Do not let your heart be troubled, trust in God the Father, trust also in me (John 14:1)

A pastor who ran a church on the South coast of England received a phone call. There was a family who would like the pastor to call on their daughter who wanted to put herself right with God as she only had a short time left to live.

He dropped everything and drove to the address. It was a large house and the door was opened by a woman dressed in a black and white servants uniform."

"Do come in pastor," she said. He thought her face was familiar but was more intent on seeing the woman who was in need. "Please follow me, pastor", she said and they went up a flight of stairs to the floor above, walked to a door and stopped outside. She went in leaving him for a moment then she quickly reappeared, "Please go in."

He entered a spacious room and there before him was the woman sitting up in bed, looking pale and very poorly.

"Please do sit down" she said, speaking his name. As he did so, he thought she looked around her early thirties.

"I had a phone call saying, you want to put things right with the Lord."

"Yes, what do I have to do?" she asked.

"You don't need to do anything, but you do need to say the sinners prayer, confessing you are a sinner," he replied.

The woman looked concerned. "But I don't have any sins to confess," she said.

"The Bible clearly says that all have sinned and come short of the glory of God, that is why God sent Jesus to die in our place, so we could be forgiven."

"But you're not listening to me! I have not committed any sins, I have lived an exemplary life, so I have no sins to confess," she insisted.

"I feel sure you have lost your temper at some time, or said things you have regretted, that's sin. Wrong thoughts are also sins."

"You're saying I'm a sinner in the same way as a thief or a murderer?" she asked.

The pastor looked at her. "Big or small, it's all sin in the sight of God. Jesus said, I am the way the truth and the light, no-one can come to God but through me."

She thought for a moment, and then said, "Thank you for coming pastor, but I'm not going to be classed alongside common thieves and murderers to get into Heaven. Goodbye!"

The pastor quickly left the house.

The girl who let him in the house had regularly attended his Sunday evening church service. She had overheard what had been said. Later that same night, she went to see the sick woman. She found her crying, so she held her in her arms, and crying with her, the maid was able to talk with the sick girl like she had never done before.

The servant girl told the sick woman that even the Queen had said the sinner's prayer.

"Have you ever said the sinner's prayer?' the woman asked.

"Yes I have. It was me that suggested to your parents that they should ring the pastor."

"I'm afraid I let my pride over rule my heart," the sick woman admitted.

—

That young servant girl led that dear woman to salvation through the act of repeating the sinner's prayer, and at the end she said, "Now you have no more to fear, because your name is written in the Lamb's book of life."

A few weeks later the sick young woman passed into eternity.

Prayer really works

I once read about a family living in the North West of England in the city of Manchester. They were parents of a teenage boy who had become mixed up with a gang who spent their time drinking and causing trouble. He was just 15 years old and his parents were worried about the company he was keeping, so they forbade their lad from going out.

When they went to bed, he sneaked out the front door, staying out all night. In the morning they were waiting for the son to come home but he never did. Two days went by and they went to the police telling them that their son was missing. The police checked the hospitals and their police stations throughout the city but had no luck, they were asked to leave all their details and they returned home.

That night they had a talk together, and decided that they should start going back to church, where they use to go at one time. At least there they could find some support and they could get help in praying for their son's safe return. Several years passed by.

Every Christmas they waited for a card or a letter, saying where the son might be, and if he was still alive, but they heard nothing.

The loss of her son hit the mother hard and slipped into a deep depression. Her husband had to take care of her and to do so he had to leave his job. He still prayed faithfully every night for the safety of their son.

The pastor of the church and his wife would pay a visit to their home every week, to see they were alright and that they had enough income to live on. They prayed with them and on each Sunday evening a lady from the church would come over to sit with the wife, so that the husband could go to church.

It was almost twenty years since their son had disappeared, and one particular day which was his birthday, they had just finished lunch, when the doorbell rang. The husband answered the door to find it was his pastor.

"Come in pastor. What brings you here this afternoon?" He asked. The pastor said nothing.

"Sit down pastor. I'll get you a cup of tea," he said.

"I would like you to sit down, my brother," said the pastor.

The father walked back with concern written all over his face.

"I had a phone call at the church office this morning, it was from someone making enquiries about you. He wanted to know if you were still at the church, your health, and so on," the pastor explained, "I asked who I was talking with and he said he was your son and that he was speaking from a phone in London. He asked if I thought he would be made welcome if he came home to visit. His train will arrive at 3.30 so you need to get to the station, I will stay here with your wife till you return, with or without your son."

The father sat there with tears flowing down his face, "He's coming home! He's coming home!" He ran into the next room to tell his wife that her child was coming home.

Going back into the room where the pastor was still sitting, he sat down in the chair, "What shall I say to him pastor?" he asked.

The pastor pulled his Bible out of his pocket, and turned to Luke 15:1, where the parable speaks of the return of the prodigal son. He read: "Now I want you to listen to what the father did. When he saw his son afar off, he ran to him, throw his arms around him, kissed his neck, and brought him home, where he told the servants to put shoes on his feet, a ring on his finger, and a robe on his back. He told his servants to kill a calf, and make a feast. That is what you must do, so you had better get on your way," said the pastor.

He took the bus to the railway station, and from the arrival and departure times board, he saw the 3.30 train from London would be arriving at platform six in a few minutes.

When the train arrived, the doors of the carriages opened, he saw hundreds of passengers emptied out onto the platform. He looked and looked, but it was impossible to see his son. He was still watching, when a hand landed gently on his shoulder and he turned to hear a tall curly headed man say, "Hello Dad, it's me, Adam."

The father opened his arms to throw around his son's waist, because he was too short to reach his son's neck.

"You've come home to us son, let's get home to your mother. She is very ill."

In the taxi they were freely able to talk, he found out Adam had hitched a truck to London, where he got offered a job in a hotel as a night porter, by a godly man that caught him looking for food at the back in the hotel bins. He took pity on him, and give him employment.

Soon he was noticed by the management, and was made an under manager. He went to college and completed the hotel and catering course. Two years later he was the general manager of that hotel. He was now married and had four children.

"Let me tell you why I came home today," he said, "One of my sons, the oldest was taken sick, it was touch and go, if he would live or die, the pain I felt at the thought of losing him, made me think of what you and mum must have gone through when I took off, so I have taken a week off work, so I could see you both."

During that week Adam was with them, he saw a change in his mother. The depression lifted, and on the last day they all went to church together, where they gave thanks to the church members for praying so faithfully.

The faith of Paul and Silas

One of the things all Christians love to do is sing praise to God. To a born again believer it's a natural thing to do. There is nothing quite like singing praise and worship to Jesus.

We read in the book of Acts (16:25-31) that Paul and Silas were arrested and thrown into prison. Iron chains were placed around their ankles and wrists. They had been beaten, but they were not about to give in, and give up. No way.

What did they do? The Bible says that about midnight Paul and Silas started to sing hymns to God. They didn't have a church organ, or guitars or drums. All they had was their voices.

They might have been in chains, but those chains were not cumbersome, so they stood up, stamped their feet, clapped their hands, and sang. Suddenly they had music, the chains were jingling with the rhythm of their dancing and hand clapping, and there was a strange sound of glory in the cell. God was being glorified and honoured.

While they were worshipping, the whole prison was suddenly shaken by a violent earthquake. The prison doors of iron were thrown open, and every prisoner in the jail felt their chains fall off.

You see, praise and prayer are the keys to open the gates of Heaven. Praise can open doors and break chains. Praise is as powerful as prayer.

So, should you find yourself in a prison of sadness, or depression, confusion or doubts, you need to be like Paul and Silas, and exercise your faith. We should never give in, but we should continue to serve, sing praises offering worship and adoration to God.

Our praise will have the same power that threw open the doors. It will loosen the hold of whatever has been oppressing and imprisoning us.

Anyone can sing praise to God when everything in the garden is rosy and the sun is shining. But it takes a change of heart, of attitude, of surrender, to sing praises when things are not going well.

When you find you self alone and the ceilings feel like iron, and your prayers and praise seem to be going nowhere. Take heart because you have a redeemer who said, "I will never leave you or forsake you." This was not an idle thought, but a solid promise.

There is power in praise and worship. There is power in faith.

The well of salvation

With joy you will draw water from the wells of salvation (Isaiah 12:3)

In the Bible days, there were no water pipes to carry water to the homes. If you wanted water, you had to visit the village well first thing in the morning, or in the evening, in the cool of the day when the sun was low in the sky.

The well was usually located in the centre of a village. If you wanted the latest gossip, you could hear it all at the well. The well would be a place of gathering, and those arriving at the same time for the same reason would talk about the news, or hear what was going on as they filled up their water pots.

But there was one woman in a village of Samaria who would come out only in the very heat of the day to fill her water pot. She was a woman who would probably have been the centre of much of the gossip that was spoken about. She was a woman of 'ill repute,' a pariah in the community. This is why she would usually go to the well when no one else was there.

However, on this one occasion someone else was there at the well. His name was Jesus. As she pulled the water from the deep well, the stranger asked would she give him a drink of the cool water. She asked why would he, a Jew, ask for water from a Samaritan woman? Socially, a Jew would have no dealings with the Samaritans.

Jesus answered her:

"If you had known the gift of God and who it is asking 'give me a drink' he would have given you living water." (John 4:10)

The woman said to Jesus. "Sir, you have nothing to draw with, and the well is very deep. From where do you get this living water?"

Jesus answered, "Everyone who drinks of this water will thirst again, but whoever drinks of the water that I shall give him will become in him a spring of water welling up into eternal life."

The woman said to Jesus. "Sir, give me this water, that I may not thirst, nor come here to draw."

At this point Jesus confronted the woman about her life style. They had a conversation about her several marriages. "You have had five husbands and the one you are living with now is not your husband," He pointed out.

The truth shocked her and she replied: "I perceive that you are a prophet. I know the Messiah is coming and when he come he will show us all things."

Jesus replied to her, "I who speaks to you, am he."

That woman went away rejoicing. She had been to the well to find water, but instead she met Jesus and had found her salvation.

Have you been to the well of salvation? Have you met Jesus? Did you come away with salvation?

I trust and pray that if you have not yet received this free gift of eternal life you will go to the well of salvation. If you do so you will never thirst again.

Singing in harmony

I sing in a choir, and the musical director will often point out to choir members that you can often only hear those around you singing, but, being out at the front, he can hear everyone; each section, every word.

Sometimes he will say "If you all keep your eyes on me, do what I'm asking you to do, I can bring a sound out of you all, that is something so sweet, so tender, so thrilling, that it will bring a smile to my face."

When I hear the harmonies of united voices, it is thrilling to my ears.

We can learn a lot from this, because as Christian believers we sometimes think, we are the only one doing anything for the Lord Jesus, or just the few of us we can hear around us.

But we only see what's going on close at hand, we don't see the greater picture. However, if we keep our eyes on the Lord, and listen to what He says, doing what He instructs, we may see a smile on His face, then we will know we are doing the right thing.

We shall see that we are part of a far bigger family and, with our combined efforts in harmony, we can cause a smile to appear on the face of our Lord.

In the world, not of the world

We are sure that we live in union with God and that
He lives in union with us, because He has given
us His Spirit. (1 John 4:13)

A ship doesn't sink because it is on the water. It sinks because
of the water that gets inside it. In the same way, many
Christians fail to live as they should, not because they are in
the world, but because of the things of the world have entered
into them.

We don't fail to produce the fruit of the Holy Spirit because
we live in a sea of corruption but because corruption has
gotten into us.

It can happen to us without us noticing. It can creep up in on
us. One time we were dedicated to following Christ, we
surrendered our will to God. But little by little the polluted
waters of the world have been allowed to seep in.

We become preoccupied with the things of the world rather
than the things of Christ. We now look on things and hear
things, we would never have bothered with, when we first
found salvation. But now things of the world have seeped in.

Most ocean-going ships have bilge pumps that are running
continuously, removing the water that finds its way inside the
hull. As Christians, we too need to keep the pumps of
repentance running, and repair any holes that may appear,
plugging them with the truth of God's word. We must not
allow the things of the world to seep in and sink our ship.

We should remember we are in the world, but not a part of it.
(John 17:16)

Living waters

John 7:38 says this: *Whoever believes in me, as Scripture has said, rivers of living water will flow from within them.*

There is an old chorus: *There is a river, that flows from God above. There is a fountain that's filled with His great love.*

God's love is truly like a mighty river, because it flows continuously and will never stop flowing. Its powerful cleansing process is mighty to save, mighty to change whosoever steps into its flow.

It starts at the very source of God's overwhelming love, bubbling up out of a fountain that is flowing down from the heart of God the Almighty, that river of grace is growing deeper and wider, deep enough for the lost to swim in. This endless supply shall never cease its flow.

Some might try to block its progress or to restrict its passage, but they labour in vain. Many on the earth over the years have attempted to stop this mighty river of God's love that is reaching out far and wide to the lost and needy, but it keeps on flowing.

There are shallow areas where those that cannot yet swim in its fullness may paddle in its wake, and sadly that is where so many are today, playing in the shallow waters. Yet the Lord would have us to swim in its fullness, to feel the mighty strength of its flow and the power of its moving.

The river of life is there for all to experience. We can step in it and enjoy it, or we can ignore it, but it's always flowing, and is fully available to all who call upon the name of Jesus.

El Adem

El Adem was once a Royal Air Force air station. It's about 16 kilometres south of the city of Tobruk, in Libya. When I was based there just after the war, in the 1950s I made friends with another Christian, a Scot who was a driver on the base.

We found a Salvation Army Red Shield canteen in the ruined city of Tobruk. On our way from our unit we had to pass the giant military cemetery where all the casualties from the battles that were fought there, in the 1941-42, are buried.

The man in charge of the cemetery was an ex Scottish Army warrant officer called Jock. He saw us go by, asked if we wouldn't mind picking him up each Sunday so he could down to the army base in Tobruk and meet up with friends for a beer. On the way down each Sunday, we would call in and pick him up.

On the driveway from the road to the entrance, there was planted on each side of the driveway a row of Scottish fir pines, brought all the way from the UK and planted there, to bring a touch of home for those fallen heroes.

After a few weeks, I noticed those trees were showing signs of losing their green colouring. They were beginning to turn brown around the edges.

I mentioned it to Jock, and he said he was aware of it, but didn't know what to do because he said he had them watered every week. I suggested he should dig one up and examine the roots.

He mentioned it to the engineers at the army base and they arrived the next day with a bulldozer. They wrapped a blanket around the trunk of one of the trees, then placed chains around the blanket, so it would not damage the trunk in any way.

They slowly lifted that tree out of the sand, only to find, the roots were still encased in the steel fuel drum when it had been transported from the UK.

Seven or eight years earlier, they were able to cut the steel drum open, removing it. They did the whole driveway within a couple of days, placing them back into the ground again where they slowly returned to their rightful colour, and later began to thrive and grow.

It was some years later I was leading an evening service in our church. In my home city of Plymouth. I was prompted by the Holy Spirit to tell this story, and to add to it. The message of the story is that those trees were dying because they were restricted in their growth. Their roots were bound, and if something had not been done they would surely have died.

I had to proclaim that there were some in that congregation who were like those trees. They were bound up in sin and doubt, unable to grow or to expand in their service for the Master. Their faith was being stifled.

Because they were bound in some way or other, they needed to pull themselves clear of what was holding them in bondage, restricting their growth. They needed to cut it away, to be free from it, and only then they would they see an improvement. Then they would witness the majestic growth in their lives. To be free is to feel positive in the things of God.

If you are reading this, you may find it is speaking to your heart. Do you feel you are bound with some hidden sin? May I suggest that now is the time to make the change. Jesus, said:

Cast all your burdens upon me, and I shall give you rest. Come unto me all you that are heavy laden and I will give you rest, restore you, comfort you and establish you. (Matthew 11:28)

The lost glove

When out for my walk one morning, I saw a little girl's glove that was laying in the wet mud on the side of the road. I walked a few places on when I saw a mother with a little girl about three or four years old.

They appeared to be looking for something, and I noticed she had only one glove on her little hands. It was the same as the one I had seen in the wet mud I reached down to pick up the muddy glove. "Is this what you're looking for?" I asked holding it up. The little girl's face lit up, "Mummy there it is!" she said, pointing.

It was soaking wet, so I put it in my hand and squeezed the water out of that little glove, before handing it back to her. She took it a with a satisfied smile and she held it to her chest, so pleased to have it back.

Her mum said "Say thank you to the gentleman." She did.

That little girl and the lost glove gave me a picture of the prodigal son, she was like the father looking for his wayward son. When I gave it to her she held it tight to her, just as the father did in the story of the prodigal son.

He ran to his son, kissed his neck, and called for shoes for his feet and a ring for his fingers, and so much more, because he had found that which he was lost and treasured. It was just like the little girl who had loved and treasured her lost glove.

I'm sure God puts little things like this in our ways, to cause us to think about Him. If you have a child that has run away, or you know of someone whose child has done that, don't give up on them. Keep praying for them, and keep watching out for them.

And when they come home, love them, hold them to your heart like the little girl did her glove. Prayer is the most powerful thing in the Christian armoury for building up our faith.

What do you see?

The Lord said to me one day "Look out of your window. What can you see?" I looked and I saw the trees and bushes in my garden, stripped of their foliage, asleep till the spring sunshine warmed the earth again to give them new life and vitality. Then these thoughts came to me:

God's message went on, "There are so many of my flock who have gone to sleep like the trees before you, who have left my love, for the pleasures of this world. These pleasures will only last for a short while. I am a gracious and forgiving God. I will come again when they call upon my name for help. I will come back into their ruined lives, to give unto them new life, eternal life.

"My warmth will energise them into the work that I have set before them. The warmth of my love will cause them to be bold and, like your trees, they will grow and send new life into their branches. This will create a safe haven for people, much like the trees can become a covering or a safe haven for birds.

"Just as the spring sunshine warms the earth causing new life to awaken in the trees into further growth and energy, so I will cause my Church to expand, to growth and produce new life, the souls of the lost will be revived, recharged into activity. Be ready for the sudden growth, not only in others, but also in your own heart, life and ministry."

If we don't leave the past in the past, it will destroy our future. Let's live for what today has to offer us, not what yesterday has taken away.

Faithful servant

Let us hold fast the profession of our faith without wavering, for He is faithful that promised (Hebrews 10:23)

Two brothers both served and loved the Lord Jesus as their Lord and Saviour. One brother was called to preach as a local preacher, in the wilds of the county of Yorkshire, where the churches were often in isolated communities in the rugged hills and dales.

A problem was that he was not a driver. However his younger brother was, so his brother drove him around. The team went on for a number of years, preaching all over the county and beyond. Then one evening, unfortunately, their car was involved in an accident and both men were killed.

There came the day, when the two stood before the Lord. Jesus said to them, "Well done, good and faithful servants. You have been faithful in your ministries, and I want to reward you." He called the preacher to him. Together they walked to the top of a mountain, looking down on the scene below then Jesus said: "My child, do you see that town down there? I want you in My name to administer over it."

The preacher thanked the Lord and walked away. Jesus then called the younger brother to him, and showed him a great city on a hill, and declared, "I want you to administer over that city."

The younger brother said "Lord, you should understand that it was not I that did the preaching but my brother. All I ever did was the driving, surely Lord, there has been a mistake. My brother should have the largest reward."

"There is no mistake, my son," answered the Lord, "Your silent witness won more souls into the kingdom than did all the preaching your brother did."

Paul wrote to Timothy saying: *I have fought a good fight, I have finished my course, I have kept the faith.* (2 Timothy 4:7)

Faithfulness is treasured by the Lord, honoured in the sight of God with a crown of righteousness.

Far more people have come to faith though the testimony of ordinary church members living a life of Christ. Many will not see the Saviour in the spoken word, but they will see Christ in the lives of the saints who have had a change of life through a personal encounter with Jesus Christ.

Can the lost see Christ in my life, and in your life today? When we get to heaven we shall know for certain.

A home in Glory

When my granddaughter and her husband were in the process of changing their home for their future needs, it made me think of the unseen home that we Christians are anticipating.

We know it will be ideal for our future needs and we can be assured that it will be perfect, because it is being prepared for us by Jesus Himself.

Jesus said to his disciples in John 14:3:

"I go to prepare a place for you, I will come again and receive you unto myself, where I am, there you may be also."

How magnificent it is going to be, because those same hands that designed the universe and all that is in it, are the same hands that have prepared our heavenly home.

What a contrast to the night that Jesus came to earth as a new born baby, not to a grand palace, but a humble cattle stall, with a manger for His bed.

Some years later when Jesus started ministering, the bible records in Matthew 8:20, the Son of God had nowhere to lay His head. There will be no rough sleepers or homeless people in heaven. Everyone will be accommodated.

Think about it, our Heavenly Father so loved the world, that he sent His only Son to Earth, to be the sacrifice, why Jesus? Because the sacrificial lamb had to be pure and spotless, that is, sinless.

Only Jesus was found to be worthy to save the souls of all mankind.

For without the shedding of blood, there can be no forgiveness of sin. (Hebrews 9:22)

Jesus willingly went to die on the cross, so that we who have called upon His name shall be saved. But saved from what? We are saved from eternal damnation by receiving eternal life in Christ.

Jesus said, *In my Father's house there are many mansions. If it were not so I would have told you. I go to prepare a place for you.* (John 14:2)

That is a promise for each of us who have run the race, those who have answered the call, those who have called on the name of Jesus and bowed their knee to Him.

Those who have seen the light and confessed our sins are ready to follow the Saviour. Those who have their names written in the Lamb's book of life have a home in Glory with their name on the door.

Is there a door with your name on it? There can be! Call on the name of Jesus today, and you too will be saved. Remember, where you are living now is not a permanent home! If you belong to him, your home is waiting for you in Glory.

No condemnation

There is now no Condemnation to them which are in Christ Jesus, who walk not after the flesh but after the spirit. For the law of the spirit of life in Christ Jesus, has made us free from the law of sin and death. (Romans 8:1-2)

The death and resurrection of our Lord Jesus was a great communicator to the glories to every object on earth that has a relationship with Christ.

It gave lustre to nature, glory and inspiration to everything and everyone living on the Earth, and to those who have been moved or touched by His salvation.

It is the precious blood of Christ that gave hope to millions of lost sinners who are now standing on the battlements of Heaven instead of in the stoke holes of Hell.

The precious blood of Jesus washed us whiter than snow. It was the blood of Jesus that gave us hope, peace, and direction, so that every believer can stand before God the Father's throne, spotless, clean and acceptable in the sight of the Father of Glory.

It is not because of anything we have done, but because of what the blood of our Lord Jesus did on the cross of Calvary for all mankind. He paid for our redemption in full.

We are no longer our own, we have been purchased with a price, by the blood of the lamb, we are the redeemed of the Lord.

We can walk tall today and every day, in the knowledge that we are no longer under the yoke of the devil, neither are we under the law of Moses. We are free in God, and are no longer in the service of a sinful nature, because we have been washed clean in the blood of the lamb.

Sometimes it's good to be reminded again of where we stand in our relationship with God the father. We should be living victorious lives, because we are covered by His blood. We can walk tall with a spring in our steps, with joy in our hearts and the smile of contentment on our faces, because we are children of the King.

The glory of the cross

Christ the Messiah is referred to throughout the entire Bible. In both old and new testaments the Messiah is represented as the most remarkable and most honourable person that has ever appeared on the stage of the world. The scriptures speak of Him as a glorious Governor, the Prince of Peace, the King of Kings, a mighty conqueror and other magnificent titles of the greatest dignity. The scriptures show that His government will be extensive and everlasting, and that His glory will fill the whole Earth.

But while prophets foretell His greatness, they write also of His suffering and rejection. They show that although He was to be a glorious king, He would be a king who would be rejected and despised of men; a man of sorrows and one who was familiar with grief. (Isaiah 53:1)

About the time of his birth, the Jews were expectant with hopes of the Messiah as the great political deliverer of their nation. They were an occupied nation and they yearned for freedom from oppression and from Roman rule.

And if history may be credited, even the heathens had a notion about that time, probably derived from the Jewish prophecies, that there was a prince of unparalleled glory who would rise in the East, and in Judea in particular, who was to establish a kind of universal monarchy.

Star gazers and dignitaries came from the East to observe the birth, saying it had been foretold in the stars.

This led some to form a picture in their minds of someone who would be a political leader, very much like the glorious conqueror in the scriptures. To them He would need to be a king who the world admired, one with extensive power, with armies, a gold crown and sceptre, a throne of state, with magnificent palaces, sumptuous feasts, many attendants of high rank, an immense treasury to enrich them, and various posts of authority to confer upon on them.

But Jesus was the obverse to all of this. He was rejected by the very people he had come to save. Instead of a crown of gold he was given a crown of thorns; for a sceptre, a reed was put in his hand in derision; the throne was replaced by a rough wooden cross; instead of a palace he had no place to lay his head; instead of sumptuous feasts to others, he often went hungry and thirsty himself.

Instead of great attendants there was a company of poor fisherman; in place of a vast treasury to give them, he had no money, not enough to pay tribute without working a miracle; the reward he had to give them was to offer each of them his cross to bear.

Everything about Christ was the opposite of worldly greatness from the first to last; a manger was His cradle at birth, and He was born into poverty in a manger. He had no place to lay His head at any time in his life, not even a grave of his own, but a borrowed one at his death.

Where is all the glory that is so much extolled?

To discover this, we need faith to look through the thin veil of flesh: and then we detect under that lowly disguise the Lord of Glory, the King of Kings, the Lord of Lords, strong and mighty, a warrior mighty in battle. The heavens are His throne, the Earth is His footstool, His garments are made of light, the clouds are His chariots, the thunder is His voice. His strength is omnipotent, His riches are all-sufficient, His glory is infinite, His retinue is the host of Heaven.

This is the King we worship today, and this was a little insight into the glory of the cross, and all of it was done so that we might all be saved.

A time of anticipation

I awoke with a song on my head one morning, so as I got out of bed I started to sing what I could remember of it:

Heaven came down and glory filled my soul. There at the cross the saviour made me whole. My sins were washed away and my night was turned to day. Heaven came down and glory filled my soul.

There I was all alone singing and praising the Lord, and it lifted me higher and higher, and the joy of the Lord was so real and so fulfilling.

I have come to that time in my life where if I want to remember something, I have to write it down. That is what I did while I was writing this. It was like the Spirit of God was saying to me: ask all your friends this question:

When did they last go to the heavenly filling station to fill their tanks with the glory of His blessings? It would certainly activate their souls and boost their faith.

I certainly felt like I had this morning. But guess what, folks. We can have all the glory we require without cost, because it was all paid for at Calvary. It cost us absolutely nothing.

Then it popped into my head, that I should clean the windows of my mind, just like a car owner would clean the windscreen, so they can see through more clearly. I think what God's Spirit was showing me was that we are so involved with earthly things, that our vision has become cloudy. As for heavenly things, we are not seeing clearly ahead what God has for us to see. We need a fresh vision of what is ahead of us.

One thing is for sure – when we arrive at our journey's end the views will be spectacular, and we shall then see everything more clearly. Then we will really know what the glory of God is all about.

But right now, while we are here on earth, we have to enjoy those moments of bless when the glory of God touches our souls, when we feel the Master's presence in the midst of us and that to bless. Those moments can be very precious to us here, but when we get to heaven they will be the norm.

Perhaps you may be reading this, but you have never experienced these precious moments when the glories of heaven have ascended upon you. Perhaps you're wondering what it's all about. It's nothing new, and if we belong to Him we can all receive it.

May the blessings of Heaven be yours today.

The great I AM

And Jesus, when he was baptised, went straightway out of the water: and Lo, the heavens were opened unto him, and he saw the Spirit of God Descending like a dove, and lightning upon him. And a voice from heaven, saying, This is my beloved Son, in whom I AM well pleased. (Matthew 3:16-17)

I have seen the place where it is thought that our Lord was baptised. It was when one of a number of our group were baptized in the Jordan river. One was an older Christian lady. She waded down into waters that were not all that clean. The water was brownish in colour. She stood with the pastor in the water with a light rain steadily pouring down, and he asked her did she want to say something?

She said, "Jesus take me as I am, I can come no other way, take me deeper into you make my flesh life melt away."

Suddenly there was an opening in the clouds a searchlight of glorious sun light shone down in a beam, flooding the scene that was before us. Our Jewish guide was from Sweden, and with tears in her eyes, she remarked that she had never seen anything so beautiful in her life.

She was greatly touched by it.

We can only imagine what those watching John baptizing Jesus felt when they saw Jesus rise up out of the water, and the heavens opened above Him. The scene would have been much the same as we had seen, except it would have been the glory of God's magnificence filling the earth, declaring to the whole world in a voice like thunder, "This is my beloved Son, in whom I AM well pleased."

Moses was commissioned by God at the burning bush to go and tell the children of Israel that God had heard their cries, and would set them free. Moses asked, "Whom shall I say sent me?"

God replied "Tell them I AM hath sent you." In the scriptures, every time we read the words I AM, it is the Almighty declaring who He is now, because God is outside of space and time (Exodus 3:13-14).

As the Holy Spirit descended like a dove and alighted on Jesus, not only was He fulfilling the scriptures by going through the waters of baptism, he was also being anointed for service by the Holy Spirit of God.

Many of you will have been through the waters of baptism, but have you also received the blessed anointing of the Spirit of God? It was only when Jesus was filled with the Holy Spirit that he began to perform the countless miracles that he did. Each and every Christian should have at least one of the gifts of the Spirit that are listed in 1 Corinthians 12:4-11. But we will not receive the gifts, or know what they are until we have been anointed by God.

If we have been commissioned by the Lord, then we are required to be equipped for spiritual battle, and if you are not fully equipped you will not be of much use to God. The gifts of the Spirit enable us to do His work.

———

He must increase

Behold, now are we the sons of God, and it doth not yet appear what we shall be, but we know that when He shall appear, we shall be like Him, for we shall see Him as He is. (John 3:2)

Some years ago we went to a league of prayer meeting where two dear ladies held a prayer group in their home. We arrived there early, and the evening sun was shining directly in through the window. We sat with the sun behind us, and I heard the footsteps of one of our members, Jimmy, as he entered the room. I said "Good evening Jimmy." He looked toward me and said, "I can hear you Ken, but can't see you because of the sun."

I replied immediately, "Oh Jim, if only it were true, that you could not see me, because of the Son in me."

You see the deeper and longer we dwell in the presence of the Son of God, the more others will see Jesus in us, and the less they will see of us.

When Moses went up the mountain to speak with God, the glory of the Lord touched him to such a degree, that he had to cover his face, when he came back down, because his face shone with the radiance of God. It was as bright as the midday sun, so the children of Israel were unable to look on him. Moses' face was glowing with the power and glory of God.

John 3:30 says He (Jesus) must increase, but I (John) must decrease.

That is what we should all be striving for, to be more like Jesus, and less of ourselves, reflecting the light of our Lord and Saviour. If we spend more time with our Lord, we too will shine with His presence, and the world will see Christ in us, the hope of glory.

We use to sing a Graham Kendrick song: *"Shine Jesus shine, fill our hearts with the Father's glory, blaze Spirit blaze set our hearts on fire."*

When I first got saved 66 years ago, the RAF men I served with at the time saw an instant change in me. My whole persona took on a new character. I was shining brighter, and my attitude had changed. I no longer felt the need to swear, and I was now able to control my bad temper.

The guys that didn't like me before, now wanted to be my friend. I was a changed man, because I had been with Jesus. I was reflecting His glory and everyone could see it. I'm afraid I have lost a lot of that shine today, because I have grown old and retired, but there is still a glow! Believe me there is still a glow.

Are you shining today? Can those around you see a difference in your life? If you're not shining brightly enough, you might need to spend more time in the presence of God, taking advantage of having some of Heaven's sunshine on your face, recharging your batteries.

During the many years I have been a Christian (I was saved on the last Sunday of 1951), I have had the honour and privilege of meeting many men and women of God. Sadly most have now been called home. But in many of them, you could see they had been with Jesus. They were totally different to other religious leaders. They were such humble men and women in their manner, maturity, and motives. They *lived* Christ, their lives focused on the Holy Bible. They only spoke one subject – Jesus Christ, and Him crucified. They only had one aim – purity of heart.

Ruth and I were once privileged to attend a double wedding of two young ladies from our church who married two brothers. The reason we were asked to their wedding was because one day they came to our house. They wanted to be prayed over, because they wanted to meet Christian men but couldn't find any. Ruth and I prayed over them. Many months after our prayers, they returned to church one Sunday evening to show us their engagement rings.

Both ladies were nurses and they heard of a farmer whose wife was seriously ill with cancer. Every weekend when they were off duty from the hospital, they would go to that farm many miles away, to care for the farmer's wife, so the husband could rest. Whilst there, they would go to the village church in the evening and it was there they met the two brothers and fell in love.

So we were privileged to attend their wonderful double wedding, where they danced down through the church. Later we went to the reception, and the vicar that performed the wedding ceremony was sitting opposite me. We introduced ourselves to each other and the first question he asked me was, "When did you give your life to the Saviour?"

We sat there for a couple of hours and the subject never wavered, it was always about the Lord. He was a man of God, engrossed in the work he was commissioned to do.

The scripture above has something very special about it. Yes, all scripture has something special about it, but here it's the verse that says:

"When Jesus appears, we will be like Him."

When did we last spend time with the Lord? Not our ten minute prayer meeting, but a long period of an hour or more in His presence, soaking in the purity and holiness of the Master's nature.

You see, the longer we spend with Jesus, the more we will be like him and, we will see Him like he is. And when we do, those you meet will think in their hearts and minds: "They have been with Jesus."

I have met some who tell me they had seen the Lord, but occasionally I have my doubts.

When I have seen those who really have been with the Lord there is no denying it, there has been such a change in their lives, their whole character is changed, their outlook on life and their countenance has had a makeover, they have obtained an inner peace, and all who see them will say, "They have been with Jesus."

Are you wanting a change in your heart and life, spend more time in His presence seeking the face of Jesus, then like Paul on the road to Damascus, you too will have a life changing experience.

Can others see Jesus in you?

Looking through some old song books I saw a song I used to sing years ago, it was called 'Can others see Jesus in you?' It was written as a reflection of the verse in the book of Acts:

When they saw the courage of Peter and John and realised that they were unschooled, ordinary men, they were astonished and they took note that these men had been with Jesus. (Acts 4:13)

If we have spent time with Jesus, then those we meet will see and feel the difference.

When I read through the words of that song again it became a challenge for me. I had to ask myself the question, can people see Jesus in me? In Acts 11:26, it was said that of the disciples were first called Christians at a place called Antioch. Christian means 'Christ like'. They were called Christians, because the people saw they had been with Jesus. Why was that? Because they had been anointed with the Holy Spirit and they had received God's grace.

The evangelist Smith Wrigglesworth was such a godly man he only had to be near someone and they became affected. This was true even though they may never have met him before.

He was once on a train in South Africa, sitting in the carriage with a complete stranger. Not a word had been exchanged, but soon the stranger fell on his knees and said, "Sir, you make me feel ashamed." The Spirit of God was reaching out, and they could see Jesus in that servant of God.

I once spoke with a man at a bus stop. He asked what I did in life. I told him about my time in the RAF, but nothing about my Lord and King. What an opportunity I missed for the master. He didn't see Jesus in me.

Can people see Jesus in me? Can they see Him in you?

I think it will make all of us ask that question.
"I gave me life for you. What have you given for me?"

The glory of God in you

Did I not tell you that if you believed, you would see the Glory of God? (John 11:40)

The glory of God is in you, if you belong to Him. To the world the 'glory of God' might be ascribed to 'mother nature' - a magnificent sunset or sunrise, a rainbow in the sky after rain, the sight of a beautiful landscape, perhaps hearing sweet music or seeing a snow-covered valley, a new born child, a thunderstorm, and so much more. To those living without Christ, this is true.

But to Christians it is the evidence of the glory of God. To the Christian believer, the glory of God has to be so much more, it's being at one with God in an intimate way. It is having faith to believe beyond the invisible. It's hearing the voice of God speaking to us inside our souls.

It is when we feel his very presence surrounding us. God's glory is whispering a prayer and knowing that God will answer it.

God's glory is knowing the will of God for you and your earthly mission. It is witnessing the supernatural happenings before our very eyes.

God's glory is seen in those beautiful occasions when we are at one with Him, when the stillness of His Holy presence is like a sheet of comfort surrounding us that you are so close that you feel that you can reach out and touch the face of God.

The glory of God is when believers let go, and let God take the helm.

It's His abiding peace that passes all understanding, that comes from being one with God, through Jesus Christ our Lord and saviour (ask anything in my name and my Father will do it).

God's glory is what raised Jesus from the dead, that gave sight to the blind, speech to the dumb, mobility to the lame, and salvation to the lost. The Bible says: *Come unto me all ye that are heavy laden and I will give you rest.* (Matthew 11:28)

It's abiding in the grace of God's forgiveness that allows us to feel free from the penalties of our sins. It's witnessing Heaven's power on earth.

What am I trying to say to you today is that the glory of God for Christians, is to rejoice in His Holy presence, so that each and every one of us should feel we are aliens here on earth. This world is not our home, but we should be so full of the glory of God, that wherever we are here on earth, it should feel like a little bit of heaven.

When He comes

The voice of him that cries in the wilderness, prepare ye the way of the Lord, make straight in the desert a highway for our God. Every valley shall be exalted, and every mountain and hill shall be made low: and the crooked ways shall be made straight, and the rough places plain: And the Glory of the Lord shall be revealed, and all flesh shall see it together: for the mouth of Lord hath spoken it. (Isaiah 40:3-5)

What a wonderful scripture this is. It's talking about the return of our Lord to this Earth. The first part is for each of us that are true believers (that we should prepare ye the way of the Lord).

We should be ready for His coming. It means preparing our hearts, our thinking, and our lives. Everything is pointing to the return of our Lord and saviour. At the last supper, as he spoke about the Holy communion, Jesus said to his disciples, "Do this in remembrance of me, do it as often as you meet until I return." This is just one of many hints that Christ will return.

Remember when the disciples were looking up to Heaven, watching to see where the Lord Jesus had gone, the Angels said, "Why are you looking for Jesus? He will return in like manner that he went" so we know our Lord will return to the holy land, where he ascended back to his Heavenly father.

And He will return in a similar manner, when every eye will behold him, and every knee will bow and every tongue will confess that Jesus Christ is Lord of all, to the glory of God the father. (Philippians 2:10-11)

And the scripture we read at the beginning is the condition the Lord is expecting from us before He returns, just as it is stated here in the scripture. When the highways are straight in the desert. I can assure you that the highways are ready.

Because without really knowing Jesus is coming soon, the Israelis have made wonderful desert highways, just like this scripture has declared, miles and miles of them. To do so they have had to level the valleys, and they have removed the tops of mountains to fill the valleys. The rough passes have been made smooth, and everything is ready for the arrival of our Lord Jesus.

We read in verse 5: *And the glory of the Lord shall be revealed.*

That is to say our Lord will show himself to the whole world, where every eye shall behold him.

In conclusion, the Bible says the mouth of the Lord hath spoken this. Are we ready for his return? And what about our loved ones, are they prepared for his appearing?

The way is ready, the stage is set, the cast is prepared. And we are waiting for the main star Himself to make his appearance. And when He does, we can expect to be snatched away

Are you ready?

Can you not hear that voice still echoing across the corridors of time? It is still repeating the same message.

Prepare the way of the Lord, make ready the desert highway (Isaiah 40:3-5)

Many, if not all, have been told that the Lord is coming soon, so we should ask ourselves the question, "Are we ready for His appearing?"

It is plain to see that many are not. If you are reading this message, can you say with all honesty that every member of your family is fully aware that Jesus is coming soon? Have they said the sinner's prayer, and accepted Christ as their Lord and Saviour?

For my immediate family most are all members the family of God, and those who are not, are fully aware of the circumstances concerning the Lords returning. However, I'm not certain about other more distant relatives or where they stand concerning their personal salvation.

If any members of our families are unaware of our Lord's returning, then we are not ready.

We who are saved and redeemed are the shepherds of the flock (family) and our commission is to care for those that have been assigned to us. We are to see they are safe and cared for, they have become our responsibility. So it's up to us to declare that the Lord is coming soon. Should they want to come with us into the Kingdom of Heaven, then they too must get ready by accepting Christ as Lord and saviour.

The scripture in Isaiah says we should make ready the highway for his coming, for only then will the Lord make His appearance. You may have your own ideas about what this portion of scripture is saying to you.

Personally, I see the highway as the church, the bringing down of the mountains, and filling in the valleys might mean bringing all Christian denominations onto the same level, doing away with denominations.

Also, we read straightening out the crooked ways and making rough places smooth. I believe this means we must stop arguing over petty differences and disputes we may have, especially those that run between various denominations.

There is only one true Church, and that is a Church that has Jesus at its head. Only when unity of the Church occurs, will we see the glory of the Lord being revealed to us openly and for everyone to see it. Every eye will see Jesus in all His glory, the saved and unsaved alike.

When our Lord departed this Earth, the disciples were gazing into the clouds and an angel said, "Why are you looking at the clouds, Jesus will return in the same manner He left." (Acts 1:11)

When the redeemed, His Church, meet the Saviour in the air, the unsaved will be doing the very same thing, looking for loved ones, in the clouds.

Blessings and peace

For I will pour water on him who is thirsty, and streams on the dry ground (Isaiah 44:3)

The blessing of the Lord it maketh rich, and he addeth no sorrow with it (Proverbs 10:22)

One morning, I was up early, so I walked to the supermarket across the bridge, did my shopping, on the way back I saw this elderly lady she had a walking stick, she was looking around like she was confused.

I asked if she was alright, she smiled at me, "Yes, thank you. I'm trying to get across the bridge to the bus stop, on the other side of the road, I'm not sure of the way to get onto the bridge."

"I'm going that way love, we can walk together," I said, having both my hands full so I could not hold her arm.

I would normally walk at a quicker pace, because I need the exercise, but, because she was an elderly lady, I walked at her pace. She informed me that she had come on the normal bus, so she now needed to get to the other side of the road, to catch the bus home.

As we walked side by side, she said , "It's much easier than I thought it would be."

"It's because you have a companion to walk and talk with," I said.

When we arrived at the other side of the bridge she knew where she was, so I said, "Nice meeting you."

"My name is Mary," she said, and I responded, "Goodbye Mary, we may meet again, the Lord Bless you."

I walked away, and arriving home, I sat down with a cup of tea, and started to read my Daily Bread. The first thing I read was 'whenever you bless people in my name, I myself will bless them.' (Numbers 6:27).

The Holy Spirit had brought this to my attention. So I thought I would highlight some of the points that the writer of Numbers was trying to put across to the reader.

God's word is always impregnated with life, wisdom, truth, power, and potential. When God spoke the words "Let there be...." every word that comes from his mouth contains the power to create.

It contains every promise God has ever made, and contains the seed of its own fulfilment. God's word cannot fail once we are aware of this truth.

The words 'God bless you' become loaded with activated power, so by speaking it to others, it releases God's blessing into their lives. When we say "God bless you" the power of God backs you up.

The Scripture explains it, "Whenever you bless someone in My name, I Myself will bless them." This is worth digesting and remembering. You are only the messenger! God is doing the delivery through you. How precious is that?

———

The Word of God on your lips is power. It is a word of action.

Once you deliver the blessing in words, God is delivering it in reality.

When you meet someone and say, "How are you?" It's an expression of courtesy and care, and when you say, "Have a nice day," you sincerely mean it. However when you say, "The Lord bless you," and you understand the scriptural truth behind those words, you will know that God's blessing can change that person's life forever! It should become a habit for Christians to bless others.

I remember a minister who travelled to Norway during the 1950s. He asked a young lad if he could point out the way to the nearest church. The lad did so, then said "The Lord bless you sir."

That blessing from that young lad, the minister said, did more for him at that moment than all the preparation and prayers that had been made by him.

He knew that God's blessing was upon him and his preaching.

Do we feel cut off from God's blessings?

Yes, this can happen in our spiritual life, when there is a blockage in the flow of God's grace through us. It happens when we find there is no longer any joy, and we are beginning to feel a hardness in our soul, when there are difficulties in our prayer life, when we read the Bible and God's word is no longer speaking to us, our hearts become hard as stone.

We start to envy those who are still enjoying the blessing and we find faults in those around us. All this is because we have allowed our thoughts to concentrate on the blockage rather than the cause of the blockage, or the one who can restore the flow.

It may only be a small thing that is causing the blockage, however it is cutting off the flow of the source of the joy of our salvation.

King David, called out to God, *"Lord return to me the joy of my Salvation."*

If we want to remove the blockage then we have to go to the source, that's where it all began for us, At the Cross of Calvary that is the source of blessing for all our needs, Christ Is the answer to our every need.

Then you will notice, when we take our eyes off the blockage looking to the Saviour, that the blockage is no longer there, and the blessings have started to flow freely again.

It's like when we become unwell, and we dwell on the

sickness, taking our eyes off the Lord. We can often become so focused on our symptoms we can't see or hear the Healer.

The important thing is never to allow anything to come between us and the Lord Jesus. No emotions, no experience, no tragedies, nothing must separate us from the love of God.

Once we take our eyes off Jesus, and focus on the storm, we will be like Peter on the water, who took his eyes of Jesus and began to focus on the storm. He began to sink and we will too.

The scriptures declare, *"He that believeth in me, out of his innermost being shall flow rivers of living waters."* (John 7:38)

Is the river of joy still flowing freely in you today, or is there a blockage that needs to be released?

Or perhaps you have never received the full blessing of God's love. Maybe you are not familiar with the flowing of God's grace in your heart and life.

Let me tell you, if you have been to the Cross and have accepted Jesus as your Redeemer and Lord, then you should have already have received God's blessings. Just like the show breads in the temple, which were fresh every morning, so we too can expect fresh blessings from Him every morning.

You should have experienced the redeeming flow of God's grace in your hearts and lives. We need to keep the channels free and flowing to receive all that God has for us. And we do that by keeping our eyes on the Master and never letting him out of our sight, then we will not stray away and cause a blockage.

May God's blessings be on you today, may His eternal joy be flowing on you and through you, causing you to reach out to others that are not yet aware of God's calling.

It is well with my soul

We read this verse: *Grace be to you, and Peace from God the Father and from our Lord Jesus Christ.* (Galatians 1:1-3)

When we have the sort of peace that we are talking about here, not only is it peace of the mind, but it's also peace of the soul.

So often when we fail the Lord, or wander down the wrong pathway, we find we are in possession of a troubled soul. It feels as though our soul has been bruised, it feels so painful, because we are full of regrets and we are sorrowful. We look at the bruised area and the darkness that's there, but when you look again later you find that it's gone. Christ has cast the misdeeds into the deepest sea, to be remembered no more, why is that? Because Jesus delights in giving mercy. His heart is full of love, and His shed blood paid for us all at Calvary.

That peace is still powerful and available to us – the peace that passes all understanding. (Philippians 4:7)

There is a wonderful old hymn called It is well with my soul. It begins:

When peace like a river attendeth my ways, when sorrows like sea billows roll, whatever my lot, He has taught me to know, it is well, it is well with my soul.

It was written by Horatio Gates Spafford, a man who had lost everything. Firstly, much of his wealth was lost when the properties he owned in Chicago were destroyed by the great fire. Soon afterwards he lost all four of his daughters in a ship wreck. Only his wife survived the tragedy.

Sometime later, as Spafford sailed from America to Europe, the captain of the ship stopped the vessel over the very spot where the ship sank. After that moment of remembrance and grief, Spafford went to his cabin to be alone with his God. It was there he was able to write the words of the hymn, 'It is well with my soul.'

How was he able to write such wonderful words after what he had been through? Only because he was at peace with God and at peace with his own soul. He was expressing his faith that God was still in control.

I trust and pray that all of you reading this can say, yes, I have this peace in my mind and it is well with my soul.

A rose on the ground

Crucified laid behind a stone, you lived to die rejected and alone, like a rose trampled in the ground.

My wife Ruth and I were walking through a supermarket and there on the floor was a rose bud, that had fallen on the floor from some ones bouquet of flowers.

Ruth stooped down and carefully picked it up. She carried it home and placed it in a saucer of water. It reminded us of those words of that chorus. "Crucified, laid behind a stone." We were not surprised when three days later that red bud burst out into a perfect rose.

It reminded us that after three days in the tomb, our Lord and Saviour burst forth from the grave, because death could not hold Him.

The grave could not imprison Him, the devil could not destroy Him. The devil was a defeated foe, and today, he is still defeated.

At Christmas we celebrate the birth of our Redeemer.

As Jesus broke forth from the Tomb on the first Easter morning, so did our Lord Jesus burst forth from Mary's womb into new life. On that first Christmas night, in a cattle shed, with the choirs of angels overhead, singing and celebrating the birth of the Son of God. Sent by the Father in Heaven to redeem the lost, to set the captives free, promising eternal life to all who believe and call upon His name.

Making a new year's resolution is easy enough to do. The difficult part is keeping to it and being true to one's promises.

We read in the Bible of where the voice of God spoke to Moses, commissioning him to lead the children of Israel out of Egypt and take them to the promised land that God had given to his children through Abraham. He also gave Moses a set of rules that they, the children of Israel should have to keep like a resolution. One such rule was that they should worship one God and one God only.

There came a day when God called Moses to come up to the top of mount Sinai, where he would meet with God, who would hand over two tablets of stone that God had written on with his finger.

Moses was on that mountain for forty days, and during that

time the people became restless and then rebellious. They made a golden calf that they could bow down to and worship.

Their true God who had set them free from the slavery of Egypt. He was the one who had made a way for them safely across the Red Sea, maintaining them through the wilderness with water, and food sent from Heaven that was there fresh each and every day. He was a God of promise, who never failed to do what he said he would perform. But still they disobeyed Him.

When Moses came down from the mountain, he found his people worshiping the golden calf. They had given no thought about honouring or worshiping the only true God, who had done so much for them. It was easy for them at the beginning to say, "The Lord our God is one God," but keeping it up was not their strong suit. God had kept his promise, but they had broken theirs.

Do you make new year resolutions? Making them is easy. Keeping them up is the hard part because it takes commitment and faithfulness.

Resilience through faith will help us to succeed.

All things work together for good

"For we know that all things work together for good to them that love the Lord, and are called according to His purpose." (Romans 8:28)

Not long after I met my dear wife Ruth, she quoted this at the bottom of her first letter to me.

She was telling me if I was not willing to follow the Lord Jesus, like she was, then I was wasting my time.

Years later there came a time when she was seriously ill. The doctor was called, and he saw right away what was wrong with her.

She was rushed to the hospital, to be operated on as soon as possible, because she had developed a faulty heart valve. The valve had to be repaired or changed.

The surgeon came to us asking for consent to proceed with the operation. He looked at the concern on my face and reassured me with, *"For we know that all things work together for good to them that love the Lord and are called according to His purpose."*

It was our bible verse, and from that moment I knew that we need not worry. It was God confirming that all would be well. She lived for another nineteen years, and saw her grandchildren and great grandchildren. Our God is so good.

I thought I would bring out a couple of points of interest for you from that story. *For we know* that all things – this is the first point, I wish to point out.

Why do we know? We know because we know the One who knows everything, the One in whom we can fully put our trust, the One who never lies, the One who said I will never leave you or forsake you. love is nothing more than putting one's trust in another person.

In all the 67 years we were married, never once did my dear wife tell me she loved me. She would say, Love is a cheap word, true love is felt and seen, not spoken. It is so true in life today.

The word 'love' is used so freely and mostly it is worthless talk, a meaningless word thrown to the wind. The love of Jesus was shown on the cross of Calvary.

There was no need to say, I love you. We could see it and feel it.

The next thing I would like to point out is in the verse: For we know that *all things*, those two words we seem to forget that our God is interested in even the small things in our lives. We have this strange habit of only bringing the large problems to Him, but even the small things should be brought before the Lord.

I heard of a watch repairer, when he was reassembling a watch, he found a wheel was missing. He looked everywhere for it; he needed it because he had told the owner of the watch that it would be ready that day.

So in sheer panic, he went to God, "Lord, it's such a small thing to bring before you, but without it, the watch is useless, please help me."

A man who worked in the floor below was working on a diamond ring when a little watch wheel dropped on his bench, it had dropped in between the crack in the floorboards, and he had seen it. He walked up the stairs to find the man on his knees, and asked him "Are you looking for this?" There in his hand was the missing wheel.

Another closer to home story was when my wife Ruth was wearing her engagement ring while cleaning at home. She noticed that one of the small diamonds was missing from the cluster on the ring. She searched everywhere for it, and in the end she sat down praying to the Lord that would show her where it was.

She stood up, her eyes were drawn to the pocket of the apron, she always wore, and there tucked away in the bottom was something shining. It was the little missing diamond.

Next day we took the ring and the small stone to a jeweller on the Plymouth Barbican and he repaired the ring. This shows us we can take even the smallest things to the Lord in prayer.

The last point I will bring is found in the verse: *To them that love God.* I was saying earlier that love is a form of putting one's trust in another person.

To put your trust in someone you trust , it is essential, knowing them, valuing them, and respecting them, if you had a difficult situation to deal with, and you had your doubts about what to do, you would not go to any one you didn't know, you would go to a family member or an old friend, someone you know, trust and respect.

That is what these few words are saying (to them that love God) we that love the Lord, we know Him, value and respect Him, because He first loved us and gave himself for us, that we might have life eternal.

The Love of God is measureless, boundless, reaching down beyond our sinful ways, our failings, and our unfaithfulness. In spite of all we have done, He still loves us.

I go back to what my wife said all those years ago: It's not what we say that shows our love, but what we feel and see, and what we do that is important.

God so loved the world that He gave His only Son to take away our sins, and that is the real test of love. Not just saying it, but living it out every day. (John 3:16)

The artist

A famous artist had read the story of the prodigal son in the Bible, (Luke 15:11-32) and the image that came in his mind was so appealing to him, he had to paint it. What he needed was someone who could be a model for the prodigal son.

He went out into the back streets of London, seeking for the likeness of the man he had portrayed in his mind. After many weeks he saw the very man he sought. He approached a dishevelled, smelly, vagrant who had no shoes on his feet.

He had no idea how old the man was. He had a full beard, long hair, his clothes were dirty and unrepairable. He was thin, sickly and unkempt looking. The artist knew this was the individual who could model the role perfectly.

He introduced himself to the man and invited him to his studio. All the man had to do was sit still for a few hours and when the artist had finished, he would pay him a good fee. He was asked to be at the studio at one o'clock the following afternoon. The artist handed over his address card.

The next day the artist worked in his studio, getting the paints, brushes and canvasses ready. The light from the window was perfect, and all he needed now was the model. He glanced at the clock on the wall.

At one o'clock precisely there was knocking on his door, and with great anticipation, the artist run down the stairs. He opened the door to find not the model, but a young man in a fine suit shiny shoes, a neat haircut, and clean shaven.

"Can I help you?" the artist asked.

The young man handed him the artist his own address card. "You told me you wanted to paint me sir, and I was to be here at one o'clock sharp. I hope I'm on time."

"But you misunderstood me," said the artist, "I wanted you to be as you were with your sordid appearance. You're no good to me now, I wanted you as you were, in your desperate condition. Please go away, you have greatly disappointed me."

The artist closed his door.

Jesus wants you and I like we are, warts and all. We don't have to spend time preparing to meet Jesus, He will gladly take us as we are. Bad habits, sinful nature and disobedient past – he will take them and make us into something special.

We used to sing a song that puts this into perspective, "Jesus take me as I am, I can come no other way."

God can take the lowest of the low in whatever sinful state they may be, and no matter what they may have done.

Just like a gifted artist he can turn us into a priceless work of art by God's grace, transforming us from earthly rags to heavenly riches.

All you have to do is come as you are, and knocking on His door to receive His forgiveness. The Bible says knock and the door will be opened, call and He will hear and answer your cry. (Luke 11:9)

A home in Heaven

Let not your heart be troubled. You believe in God, believe also in me. In my father's house there are many mansion, if it was not so, I would have told you so. I go and prepare a place for you, and if I go to prepare a place for you, I will come again and receive you to myself, that where I am, there you may be also (John 14:1-3).

When He was here on earth ministering to the people, Jesus never had a permanent home to call His own. He lived with his parents until he was thirty, and then He left home to start His itinerant missionary work. From that moment on, He literally had no place to lay His head (Matthew 8:21).

When we think that Jesus left the magnificence of Heaven – and we can only imagine what it must have been like – to be born in a stable, it is astounding. He had nowhere to stay, and only His robe to keep Him warm, as He slept out under the stars.

He went from the splendour and grandeur of Heaven to a rough bed on the sand. Yet the bible tells us that Jesus emptied himself of Heaven's finery, to be born in human likeness (Philippians 2:7). He was God as a man.

Out of love for a lost people, he loved us so much that he left it all behind, that he might bring salvation to you and I. Jesus left behind Heaven's glory in exchange for earthly simplicity.

He was misunderstood, condemned to death on the cross of Calvary, beaten, whipped, insulted, spat upon, yet even in the last hour of His life He called upon God the Father to forgive those that nailed him to that cursed tree.

He that knew no sin became sin for us, and He did it all because of His love for the fallen race of humanity.

But thankfully the story doesn't end there.

Yes, He died, but Jesus arose from the dead just like He had promised. He was seen by more than five hundred people, alive and talking to them. Later, it was while He was talking to his disciples that he ascended up into the sky out of their sight, where he is now sitting at the right hand of God the Father in glory. It is from there that He intercedes for his followers still on earth.

One day those of us who follow Him will join Him in the glorious heavenly home that he has prepared for each and every one of us. That will be how His promise will be fulfilled, when He said, "I go to prepare a place for you, that where I am, there you may be also." (John 14:3)

We all know that we will die at some point in this life, but the important question is, where are we going to spend eternity? There are only two places we can go. To be certain of a place in Heaven, you only need to call upon the name of Jesus for your salvation. Then you will be saved, and you can be assured that your home in glory has already been prepared for you. It's that simple.

Going to church will nor save you, nor will any amount of good works. There is only one way to get into heaven, and that is by accepting Christ as lord and saviour of your life. (Ephesians 2:8-9)

The Damascus road

The apostle Paul was one of the foremost evangelists and most notable figures in the early church. He wrote much of the New Testament and established many early churches across Asia and Europe.

When we first come across Paul, he was known as Saul of Tarsus. We first read of him holding the coats of those that were stoning Stephen, a disciple of Christ, to death. The book of Acts says Saul approved of the execution of Stephen and even encouraged it. (Acts 8:1)

Saul's sole mission in life at that time was to stamp out the Christian faith, which was growing rapidly in and around Israel. He sincerely believed he was doing God's will because he considered Christianity to be a blasphemy against the beliefs of Judaism.

Later, after the stoning of Stephen, Saul continued to shout out murderous threats again those who professed to be disciples of Christ. (Acts 9:1)

Suddenly everything changed when Saul was on his way to Damascus, to arrest the Christians that had moved there.

Saul has been thrown to the ground by a great light, and was unable to see, but he heard a voice speaking to him. It was the voice of Jesus.

Saul met with the Lord Jesus Christ on that Damascus road and very soon afterwards, Saul the persecutor, was transformed into Paul the proclaimer – one of Christ's most notable evangelists. What a radical change!

Instead of shouting murderous threats he now proclaimed the Gospel message to anyone who would listen. Many years later he was taken in chains to the city of Rome, the centre of the great Roman empire. He was unafraid, because he was ready to die for his Faith.

Many years later, that is exactly he did when he gave his life for the cause of the Gospel.

The event that changed his life was the meeting with Jesus on the Damascus road. This encounter changed his life completely, and although less dramatic, my encounter with Jesus has also changed my life.

Many others down through history can claim the a similar personal transformation.

And it has been like that with of millions of people down through the ages, and is still true today. The moment Jesus meets with someone, they are never the same again..

Another thing we noticed from the moment of his conversion was that Paul saw people through the eyes of God. He no longer looked at others through his own the eyes.

Daniel 12:3 says this: *And they that be wise shall shine as the brightness of the firmament: And they that turn many to righteousness as the stars, for ever and ever.*

The author

An author was once visiting a writer's club to do a reading and book signing. Most of the audience were aspiring writers and he was determined to inspire them with a few words of encouragement on how to write a successful book.

The author spoke: "Remember that each and every one of your lives are like the book you are writing. You can only write one chapter at a time, and you can only live one life at a time.

"As you write your story, you can develop the character in your book into anything or anyone you desire. That is your prerogative."

The author was talking about book writing, but what about your own life? You are writing the story of your own life every day. Are you pleased with who you have become, or would you like to change your own character and be someone else?

What you write is a record of your life during that period, and if you think the last chapter of your book was the most fruitful, the most thrilling, where your life is the best up to the present time, remember that you are still writing a chapter now. Your life continues until the last chapter is complete.

If you are looking for a successful book, you will require a great ending so that when the story finally concludes it should bring a satisfying smile to the readers' faces.

But what about your own life's final chapter? Have you written it well? You and I will have met many people on the way, some we loved, some we didn't like one bit. Yet they have all added to the wealth and depth of each of life's stories.

And so it is in the Christian life. Many will cross our paths during our Christian lives, and some will help us, encourage and love us. But others will do the opposite. They will drain us of our peace and contentment, and make our lives a misery.

We often come to the point when we say: "Lord, why has this happened to me?" But it's all part of God's plan for you and I.

It is to build us up in our faith, to help us develop more tolerance, patience, resilience and grace. When we understand that nothing on this earth is here by chance, we see that it is all in God's purpose.

Being in the will of God we may be subjected to terrible situations, much like the story of Joseph sold into slavery by his brothers. But in all the years Joseph was cast away from his family, but he never strayed far from the presence of his God.

God took a simple lad and allowed all manner of things to happen to him, with many people coming and going in his life, some good, some bad. But all combined to create the full and interesting life story that culminated in Joseph becoming one of the most influential people in ancient Egypt.

What a way to end a chapter in a book of life! Our lives can be as interesting and fulfilling as Joseph's was, if we put our trust in God and never doubt that He knows the beginning from the end.

And that goes for the bad as well as the good times.

The salesman

Many years ago, people were always knocking on doors trying to sell things to us. They were called door-to-door salesmen (they were invariably men).

The young man at our door was no exception. He had all the patter, showing us how the device he was demonstrating was the most wonderful vacuum cleaner in the whole world.

"It's all the way from the USA, it's the world's best kept secret! You can be the owner of this phenomenal vacuum cleaner!" he enthused.

I asked the price, but he would not say. He just kept rambling on with his sales talk as he was trained to do.

"You will have a dust free house, do you know how much dust each human being can create in 24 hours?" He gave some statistics. He had all the details about this magnificent, revolutionary machine and everything it could do. "It will change your life, Sir," he kept going.

Finally he stopped to breathe, and I asked him, "What sort of vacuum do you have in your house?"

He mentioned some make of British that was commonly available anywhere.

"If this new vacuum cleaner is so wonderful, why don't you have one?" I asked.

He answered truthfully, "Because I can't afford one."

That was the only true statement that he made while he was in our house.

"Then we can't we afford it either," I said, and showed him to the door.

The salesman was well trained and versed, knowing all there was to know about the product. But he was only saying what he had been trained to say. He had no real hard and fast personal evidence of how the product performed in his own home. What he was trying to sell us was something he had never tried personally.

I guess you might be able to see where I'm going with this, in a spiritual sense.

There are those that say they are Christians, born again, blood bought, and Spirit filled. They have all the head knowledge there is to know about the Bible. However, they do not have any real hard and fast evidence of the presence of the Lord in their personal lives, or in their homes. It's all fancy talk. They are like that young salesman. They have a lot of confidence in themselves, but none in the product that they are proclaiming, because they have never truly tried it in their own homes, and on their own family.

If we are going to proclaim the gospel to those in need, we not only have to know all about it, but we need to have tried it personally, and to be able to say we have a relationship with the author.

By this I mean knowing the author of salvation. It goes beyond knowledge. His presence should be demonstrated as living within each one of us.

This is the only real evidence of Christ we ever need to demonstrate.

Only believe

Robert was someone important in the City, trading stocks and shares all day. He had no time for God and no time for his family. His god was making money and his temple was the balance sheet. He would come home late from work and after eating his evening meal, he would pull open his laptop. From then on, until he collapsed into his bed, he would have no conversation with his wife or family. Robert's wife was a Christian, so she wouldn't entertain the thought of leaving her husband.

She had married him and had vowed before God that their marriage would be for better or for worse. So, whilst he was on his computer, she would be praying in faith that God would answer her prayers of bringing salvation into their home and to save their marriage.

She was ready to go to bed one night, when Robert asked her for coffee. She made a cup for him and it down by him, and then went to bed. Robert had been so engrossed with his statistics, he forgot about the coffee, and before he had realised, he had knocked the cup sideways, spilling the hot contents all over his laptop.

His laptop sparked and emitted some odd noises. He tipped it, hoping to drain the coffee out. He frantically wiped the surface with his handkerchief, but it was too late. The damage had been done. All of his important data was lost. Robert flew into a rage and swearing loudly, he threw his laptop across the room, where it lay against a wall. The screen blinked on and displayed just two words in bold print, "Only believe."

Robert saw the words clearly, and he was shocked. They were the same two words that had been in a frame over his

Grandmother's bed. They had been the first words he had ever read. Beneath the text was where his grandmother would read Bible stories to him, and where she prayed for him.

When his Grandmother passed away, the only thing Robert wanted was that picture over the bed, "Only believe." He still kept the frame on the top of his wardrobe.

Robert fell on his knees, and felt the tears flowing down his face. He remembered the love the tenderness his gran had shown him. He felt a hand rest gently on his head, then a still soft voice speaking to him.

"It's time to return Robert, and put your trust in me. You have wandered away seeking your fortune, but now you're weary and tired from your labours. Only I, Jesus, can give you rest."

That night God answered his wife's prayers. Salvation came to the house, and their marriage was saved. Robert found a new faith in Jesus.

The next day Robert took his laptop to a specialist who was able to restore all the figures that Robert thought he had lost. He now uses that same laptop to do the church accounts.

The key message of this story? Don't allow the search for a fortune to rob you of your salvation or your relationships, or divert you from the path that the Lord has placed you on – the path of faith and trust in a Holy God.

Finding peace again

David was aged four when his Grandad moved in two doors away so that he could be near his family.

David loved to come home from school and rush eating his dinner so he could go to see Grandad. He found his grandad exciting. He could sing songs, do all manner of tricks, and helped David do his homework. Above all he could tell stories that filled David's imagination and being with his Grandad was the highlight of David's day.

When David was about eight years old, he came home from school and had his dinner, and then said, "I'm off to see Grandad."

"Not tonight David," his mother said, "Your grandad is unwell. Perhaps you can see him tomorrow."

The next afternoon David arrived home from school and found his mother crying, "Why are you crying mummy?" he asked.

"Because Grandad has gone to be with Jesus. They took him away this afternoon, so I'm afraid you will not see Grandad ever again." She hugged David.

David was very shocked by the sad news. He pushed his mother aside and raced to his room, throwing himself onto his bed.

The loss of his dearest friend was a time of great sorrow to him, it made a lasting impression on his young life. David became a sad lonely boy, withdrawn within himself, making few friends. As the years passed, he did well at school, his grades were good enough for him to enter university. It was while he was at university he saw a notice inviting students to the Christian Union meeting. He went along curious about what went on and saw there were about twenty other students attending. David lingered around in the background.

The man leading the meeting was an older person, and when it came the close of the meeting, the leader opened his Bible and started to read a story.

This made David pay attention, as it was a story that he knew so well, because his Grandad had told him this story many times. It was with a story of the prodigal son, how he took all that was due to him from his father. Travelling to a foreign country, he spent everything he had on wild parties.

Eventually he ended up with no money, and all his so called friends left him. He became so destitute he was forced to take a job feeding the pigs (something that would have been against the rules of Judaism).

He soon realised he could live a better life as a servant in his father's house, so he decided to return home. When he saw his father, he begged for forgiveness and offered to become a servant in the house. Instead, his father welcomed him home as his long lost son.

The memories of the story flooded back into David's soul. Suddenly his eyes filled with tears he sobbed uncontrollably like he had not done since that night he was told of his grandads death, those with him, tried to give him comfort, he knew none of this at the time, only that the truth and dawned on him, that he had loved his grandad but he had deserted his memory, and all the truths that he had Implanted in his heart.

That night when he had been told of his death, he had buried everything his Grandad had instilled in him. It contributed to the lack of joy and excitement in his life.

When the tears had ceased, he was able to speak again. He told the students around him how his love for his Grandad was so great, that when he had lost him, the shock being so great. Everything he had learnt from his Grandad was buried. But now it had all returned to him.

David rededicated his heart and life back to Jesus that night, like he had when he was a boy, David blossomed as a Christian. Eventually he became the President of the Christian union of that University. Living for Christ was his new found joy, and his witness drew many other students into its ranks.

It's only me, Jesus

Remember me, O Lord, with the favour you have toward your people. Oh, visit me with your salvation. (Psalm 106:4)

The church warden of a church in a city in south of the England watched a workman, dressed in dirty blue overalls, walk into the church and make his way down to the front of the church. He lowered himself down onto his knees, and was there for about ten minutes. He then got up and walked out of the church. The warden noted the time - it was midday.

The following day at the same time the man walked in again, he went through the same routine as the previous day. The warden wondered what was going on, so after a week of the man arriving always dead on at midday, he allowed himself to watch from the side to see that nothing unusual was going on.

He heard the man say "Hello Jesus, it's only Jim here, stopped by to say hello."

He said nothing more for a while. But then he said, "Goodbye Jesus, I will be back again tomorrow."

This went on every day except Sunday for about three weeks. When the church warden noticed he didn't come in. Later the church warden heard that a building that was being demolished in the next street had collapsed, and five workers were buried beneath the rubble.

The rescue team pulled the five men out from under the wreckage and raced them to the hospital. They were all injured, some worse than others. But luckily, no one had been killed.

After a few days, the sister in charge of the hospital ward heard the rescued men laughing. She went in to investigate why because they were making so much noise.

"What's so funny, gentlemen?" she asked.

One of the rescued men replied, "It's Jim, he's making us all laugh. Since we've been in here, every day at twelve o'clock, he looks toward the end of his bed, and then he holds a conversation with someone, but there is no one there. He must have been knocked hard on the head when the wall fell on us."

The nursing sister was concerned for Jim and went over to check on him.

"How are we today Jim?" she asked.

"I'm just fine, thank you sister" was his reply.

"Your work mates say you have been talking to someone at the foot of your bed. And there is no one there," she said.

"Oh, there was someone there alright. It's my friend Jesus. He comes to see me every day, at midday."

"Now why would Jesus come here to see you, Jim?" she asked.

"Because I used to go and see him in his church, but since I got hurt, I couldn't go. So now he comes here to see me."

"And what does Jesus say to you Jim?"

"He says 'Hello Jim, it's only me Jesus, stopping by to say hello.' We have a little talk, and then he leaves, saying he will be back again tomorrow."

Epilogue

I wrote that short story a few years ago for a church magazine, and it's not so farfetched as it may seem.

Many today are receiving visits from the Lord Jesus at night, in their dreams. I have read of many Muslims that have been converted to Christianity, because they have received a visit from the Lord Jesus Himself.

One of my sons, Steve, also experienced this same amazing blessing. He told us how Jesus had been to his room, he had awoken to see Him at the foot of his bed and had spoken with Him. Oh yes, Jesus is certainly real enough.

I have known of others that have seen Him, in all His glory, and their lives have been totally changed.

I haven't seen the Lord myself, but I have known His tangible presence on several occasions, and have sensed the beauty of His holiness. However, one day when I finally get to Heaven I will see Him face to face, and then I'll sing my story 'saved by grace.'

The Lord bless you.

Without faith it is impossible to please God
(Hebrews 11:6)

If you enjoyed this book, you may also enjoy reading other titles recently published by Wheelsong Books:

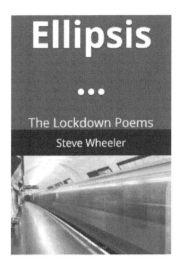

Ellipsis – The Lockdown Poems by Steve Wheeler

ISBN: 9-798666-415252

Poems written during the global pandemic of 2020 with themes ranging from heroism, depression, hope, racism and faith.

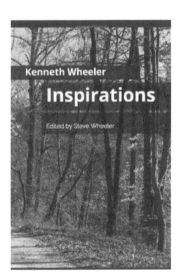

Inspirations – Poems and reflections by Kenneth Wheeler

ISBN: 9-798667-258360

Inspiration writing about faith, love, family, life and celebration of all things good. Proceeds go to Open Doors charity.

Sacred – Poems by
Steve Wheeler

ISBN: 9-798669-576806

A collection of poems
charting the author's
journey of faith, and
exploring love, hope,
failure, fear, poverty
and racism.

All titles are available for purchase in paperback and
Kindle formats on Amazon.com

Printed in Great Britain
by Amazon